8 Days with God and Man

Meditate on These Things – The Series – Book #2

8 Days with God and Man

Palm Sunday to Resurrection Sunday

Dan Needy

XULON PRESS

Xulon Press
2301 Lucien Way #415
Maitland, FL 32751
407.339.4217
www.xulonpress.com

© 2021 by Dan Needy

All rights reserved solely by the author. The author guarantees all contents are original and do not infringe upon the legal rights of any other person or work. No part of this book may be reproduced in any form without the permission of the author. The views expressed in this book are not necessarily those of the publisher.

Unless otherwise indicated, scripture quotations taken from the New King James Version (NKJV). Copyright © 1982, 1990 by Thomas Nelson, Inc. Used by permission. All rights reserved. Emphasis mine throughout.

Paperback ISBN-13: 978-1-4984-6215-0
Ebook ISBN-13: 978-1-6628-1215-6

Contents

Acknowledgements vii
Introduction. ix
Chapter One: An Irrepressible Journey 1
Chapter Two: Value in Waiting 9
Chapter Three: Passion Week – Day One, Palm Sunday 17
Chapter Four: Passion Week – Day Two, Fig Monday. 38
Chapter Five: Passion Week – Day Three, Teaching Tuesday 54
Chapter Six: Passion Week – Day Four, Silent Wednesday 68
Chapter Seven: Passion Week – Day Five, Maundy Thursday 81
Chapter Eight: Judas Iscariot, Tragedy in The Midst of Victory 101
Chapter Nine: Passion Week – Day Six, Good Friday. 112
Chapter Ten: Passion Week – Day Seven, Sabbath Saturday. 141
Chapter Eleven: Passion Week – Day Eight, Resurrection Sunday. . . 150
Chapter Twelve: Final Thoughts. 164
Notes 169

Acknowledgements

God has a way of altering our plans as we journey through life. While we often never fully know or understand the reasons why, our faith reassures us that He makes no mistakes in either His decisions or His timing.

This book is a prime example. The idea for it was birthed in an email in 2013. I started writing the manuscript in 2014. However, open heart surgery, a pacemaker, and kidney surgery put the book on hold.

I am eternally grateful to all the friends and family who prayed for me and for this book throughout the past seven years. While putting thought to paper was mostly dormant, the heart and passion for the message only grew as prayer lifted the project to God for guidance and inspiration.

Many people have encouraged us along the way. In addition, there are others who have had an integral part in the book's content and layout:

Friend and Pastor Rick Nerud provided exceptional biblical and theological guidance. I thank him for his tenacious, honest, and thorough examination of each chapter, paragraph, and word.

Friend Carol Poulton provided grammatical and punctuation expertise.

Friends Joe and Caroline Slobig meticulously aided in the proofing and editing. Their skills are acknowledged and appreciated.

My sister, Loretta Hiel, provided proofing and content skill and general advice.

Finally, my wife, Patricia, and family have provided inspiration and love unmatched during this lengthy and challenging process.

Dan Needy

Introduction

> "It is a season of grace, bringing about a communion with Christ. It is a season of blessing for all of God's people."
>
> Bishop Michael Jarrell

Now before the Feast of the Passover, when Jesus knew that His hour had come that He should depart from this world to the Father, having loved His own who were in the world, He loved them to the end (John 13:1).

In all the annals of time, in all the days, months, years, and centuries of earth's existence, there is one eight-day segment of time that changed the spiritual landscape of this universe forever. Eight short days—but a flicker of time—yet their impact cannot be erased nor diminished. Civilizations are measured by centuries. Kingdoms are measured by decades or years. Singular events have their impact— though often just for a brief moment. Yet never has such a series of events so changed the world as these scant days.

Were we to embed those eight days back onto the canvas of time, they would be reduced to obscurity. They would be suffocated and consumed by their minuteness. They would be lost in the expanse of the ages. Time itself would try to push them into irrelevancy.

But undeniably, nothing has ever realigned the cosmic disorder caused by man's fall as did these eight days. No duration of time, whether short or long, cradled events that so recalibrated the spiritual imbalance that existed in mankind. No other segment of time and no other sequence of actions has ever produced—or will ever produce—events that could so divinely repair the relationship between the holiness of God and the depravity of fallen man—except the events of these eight days.

What unfolded literally shook the earth and altered man's future forever. History has been so captivated by this speck of time that many of its days bear special names: Palm Sunday, Spy Wednesday or Silent Wednesday, Maundy Thursday, Good Friday, Easter Eve, and Easter Sunday or Resurrection Sunday.

The timing of and location of the events of these eight days were not a result of mere chance or the coming together of a perfect storm. Those who would become central characters to the story did not just happen to run into each other on the street and a crucifixion broke out. Oh, no! God, through His prophets, told the story of redemption thousands of years before it would occur, and the Hebrew people awaited that day—the day of the Messiah's arrival. Scriptures reveal forty-four Messianic prophecies and more than 350 total prophecies about Jesus—each one precisely fulfilled throughout His life, death, and resurrection. This was an event that was orchestrated before the foundations of the earth were formed, and when its time had arrived, the course of history was changed forever.

For the Jewish people, this was the time of Passover—the most sacred of celebrations. Passover was appointed by God, designed by God, and commanded by God that the Hebrew people might remember His mighty acts in bringing them out of the land of Egypt. While in terrible bondage, the Hebrew people cried out to God; God heard their cry for help and sent Moses to lead them out of captivity.

> *Now it happened in the process of time that the king of Egypt died. Then the children of Israel groaned because of the bondage, and **they cried out;** and their cry came up to God because of the bondage. **So God heard** their groaning, and God remembered His covenant with Abraham, with Isaac, and with Jacob. And*

Palm Sunday to Resurrection Sunday

> ***God looked upon the children of Israel,*** *and God acknowledged them*
>
> – Exodus 2:23-25

How fitting it is that God would choose the season of Passover to free His people again. The Hebrew people had waited and yearned for the coming of the Promised Messiah—to once again be set free from bondage. Centuries ago, it was the bondage of Pharaoh—this time, the bondage of the Romans. Surely, He would destroy the Romans just as He had Pharaoh. Had they not often cried out to be freed once more from oppression? Oh, yes! They had cried out! Would God again not destroy their enemy as He promised through the prophet Micah? *Yet out of you shall come forth to Me **the One to be Ruler in Israel** . . .* (Micah 5:2b).

That is who the Jews were waiting and longing for—the one to be ruler in Israel! No more Roman rule—no more oppression—no more bondage.

But God saw a much worse bondage than the one that was being inflicted by the Romans. God saw the very bondage of sin itself—crushing the people, destroying their lives, and robbing their joy.

However, this freedom would not be reserved for just the Hebrew people. No, it would be much larger than that—it would be spiritual freedom for all mankind! And the world rocked as a Savior rent the veil in two, removing our shackles, granting mankind freedom from sin and the opportunity to live the abundant life. Jesus Himself said it this way: *I have come that they may have life, and that they may have it more **abundantly*** (John 10:10b).

How appropriate then that Passover, the celebration God had chosen to be among the most sacred of all feasts, would suddenly become even more significant, even more sacred, even more memorable. To all who would believe in His Son Jesus Christ, God provided a way of escape—escape from the captivity of sin and the burden of the Mosaic Law. To all who would accept this "freedom" from sin, God would give eternal life. Never again will Jews celebrate Passover without the irrepressible influence of "that Passover."

For Christians, this too is a time of remembrance. They call it Passion Week or Holy Week or Easter. It is a time of remembrance of a Savior who was beaten, battered, bruised, and put to death by crucifixion, hanging on a primitive cross. It is a time when all Christianity mourns, groans, and suffers at the picture of such great punishment. Even the world is captivated by the drama of so savage and unjust a story. The volumes of books and movies—attempting to expose the horrendous details on printed page and on screen—is astounding.

But this is also a time of great celebration for Christians—the celebration of a Savior not destroyed by death but risen from the dead—the conqueror of death itself. Christians celebrate the death of Christ as well as His resurrection. Without death, there could be no resurrection, and without His resurrection, there could be no hope for mankind.

Even the world cannot escape how special these days are. Mingled with the celebration of a Savior, the world strives to minimize—yes, even deflect or deny—the Risen Savior. The world, predictably, has attempted to disfigure the true meaning and significance of the events that occurred. Secularism tries to squeeze out the spiritual meaning by making this time about anything and everything but a crucified and risen Savior. Easter is instead a time for bonnets and parades and bunnies and greeting cards. It is a time for family picnics and elaborate, over-the-top dinners. It is a time for vacations and it is time off work. For most, Passion Week does not exist. No, instead it is Easter—just another holiday—void of its spiritual impact and its wonderful message of hope.

However, regardless of the attention given or deflected or rejected, God's purposes were fulfilled at this appointed time—these eight days. His plan to save mankind would not be stopped or delayed. His Son would not be repressed. His remedy to restore fallen man would be fulfilled. And it was at this appointed time that Jesus Christ would impact the world so much that time itself would henceforth be measured from the life of Jesus Christ. BC (Before Christ) and AD (Anno Domini—the year of our Lord) would become the point from which years would be numbered in the Julian and Gregorian calendars—with the Gregorian lunar-based calendar becoming the overwhelming World Calendar.

So, what were the events that caused this blip of time to earn such prominence—to be called Holy Week, to be known as Passion Week or Easter? What happened that an entire world would be drawn—through the centuries—to worship and celebrate its events? Let us look.

Three predominate events highlighted this most busy week in Jerusalem. While much more occurred, these three events fulfilled God's perfect plan of redemption for mankind.

It started with a triumphal entry into the old city of Jerusalem. This event set off a chain of events that would fulfill all of the prophesies of a coming Messiah. *Rejoice greatly, O daughter of Zion! Shout, O daughter of Jerusalem! Behold, your King is coming to you: He is just, and having salvation, lowly, and riding on a donkey, a colt, the foal of a donkey* (Zechariah 9:9).

The crowds were filled with jubilation. The city was abuzz. The atmosphere in Jerusalem was electric. On every corner, the stage was being set for the most monumental of cosmic battles—but few, if any, knew it. No event has ever fulfilled such a wide scope of expectations— for good and for evil. Our look at this first day of Holy Week will examine its significance for its time, our time, and eternity.

The second event, a few days later, revealed a gift that would be given, and its impact would physically and spiritually shake the very foundations of the entire universe. It was a gift of love that has the power to forgive every man's sin—to all who would and will believe on His name—the name of Jesus. But this gift would not be wrapped in pretty paper. It would not produce the joy usually associated with receiving gifts—at least not immediately. It would not even look like a gift or feel like a gift. Instead, this gift would be placed on full display for all to see—high and lifted up on a crude and cruel cross of crucifixion. The landscape around would soon look more like a crime scene—and by any measure of justice, it was—than the revelation of the greatest gift ever offered. And all, who either intimately or even casually examine this event, are required to accept or reject the gift themselves.

But then, three days later, the event that became known as the Resurrection occurred, complete with a missing body and, in subsequent days, multiple appearances of the risen Savior. There would be joy, fear, and doubt. There would be accusations and naysayers and ridiculers. Some would call the Resurrection a hoax. Others would call it fraud—still others would say it was impossible.

And when these eight days were over, man was left trying to sort out what the world had just witnessed. Had the Messiah come? Or was this some terrible joke? And if this man Jesus was really the Messiah, why did He not conquer the Romans and free His people? And how could the King of Kings be so bitterly shamed by the worst form of death known—crucifixion on a cross? The expectations the Jews had for their Messiah did not fit the events just witnessed. They expected their nation to be physically freed from tyranny. But Jesus had come to give spiritual freedom to all mankind. For many Jews, even today, the flaw of misguided expectations became and is a hindrance to belief.

However, for some, the uncertainty of the past few days—days filled with mystery and confusion—would lift like a morning fog, and words spoken and events that occurred earlier would begin to take on clearer meaning.

Today, confusion still surrounds those events of long ago. For some, the reports and accounts recorded of those events never really happened—rather simply being stories contrived for deception or gain. Others today are unwilling or unable to accept Jesus Christ as the Messiah. Still others avoid the purpose of Christ's death, choosing to focus on who was at fault rather than the purpose of Christ's crucifixion. There seems to be such a desire to place the blame for the "crime." Did the Jews crucify Him, or was it the Romans or the Gentiles? Thus ignoring Jesus's own words when He said, *Therefore My Father loves Me, because **I lay down My life** that I may take it again. **No one takes it from Me**, but **I lay it down of Myself**. I have the power to lay it down, and I have the power to take it up again. This commandment I have received from My Father* (John 10:17-18).

Through the ages, and even today, biblical scholars and theologians share in the confusion. The simplistic story of salvation has been so dissected and cut into miniscule pieces for analyzation that the wonderful story of redemption misses being told. Let me explain:

There is much disagreement concerning the sequence of the events of Passion Week—the date, the time of day, and the day of the week each event transpired. It would be nice to say at a specific time, on a specific day, this is what happened. However, in trying to be historically accurate, many obstacles arise. The exact timing of an event and on what day of the week the event actually occurred those two thousand years ago is difficult, at best, to determine. To form an enlightened opinion requires:

- An understanding of both Mosaic Law and Jewish tradition concerning the Passover Feast and the Feast of Unleavened Bread
- An understanding of the Gregorian calendar
- An understanding of the Jewish calendar
- An in-depth knowledge of the four gospels—Matthew, Mark, Luke, and John

The complexities of the Jewish calendar and its differences with the Gregorian calendar add to the challenge. While the Gregorian has a twenty-four-hour day with months and days defined by lunar charts, the Jewish calendar starts its day at sundown—thus encompassing part of two twenty-four-hour days of the Gregorian calendar.

In addition, having an understanding of Jewish traditions (which often changes) is necessary. Was there one or were there two Passover Sabbaths that year? Was the crucifixion on Thursday or Friday? And what about the three days between the crucifixion and the resurrection? While the Mosaic Law may have been definitive and exact, the practice of those laws were, and are still, not so exact. For example, in Leviticus 23:4-8, we read Passover shall be a seven-day feast. For modern-day Jews in Israel, it is a seven-day celebration. But Jewish tradition allows an additional day for Jews living outside Israel to compensate for travel to Jerusalem and other factors—thus an eight-day Feast.

The gospels give us some clues—such as Matthew 26:17: *Now on the first day of the Feast of Unleavened Bread . . .* But even then, there are ambiguities as to what day of the week the "first" day is. To further challenge us, the Jewish calendar adds intercalary months every nineteen years to adjust for leap year. All these issues—and more—add to the confusion surrounding these eight days. As can easily be seen, turning back the calendar two thousand years is not so easy. And what calendar is it we are going to turn back to anyway?

Therefore, for the purposes of this book, we will follow today's commonly accepted times of the major events—Palm Sunday, Good Friday, and Resurrection Sunday. This is done to simply place the emphasis on the events themselves rather than the exact time of their occurrence and to provide the reader with a structure on which to base their study.

So, then, what is the purpose of this book?

As a devotional study, our goal is to take you back two thousand years to Jerusalem and to try to imagine what those eight days were like for Jesus the Messiah and Jesus the man. What was it like for the disciples? And how about the multitudes and the merchants and the Romans and the religious rulers? What were their days like—back then—some two thousand years ago? And what should ours be like today?

On Thursday, March 28, 2013, I sent this email to several acquaintances. It became the inspiration for this book:

Yesterday was "Spy Wednesday." It marks the day Judas received thirty pieces of silver to betray Christ. Did you think about that during your day yesterday? Sadly, I did not. I should have and prayed, but I did not.

Jesus, after spending the day in Jerusalem, traveled to Bethany and spent the night at the home of Simon the leper. There, He was anointed with fragrant oil as a foreshadowing of His burial. Even then He used the occasion to teach His disciples.

So, now it is Thursday—"Maundy Thursday." As I watched the sunrise this morning and quickly went through some of the plans for today, my mind was quickly brought to the question: "What was today like for Jesus those two-thousand-plus years ago?" If we spent the day with Him, we would see His day will be spent preparing for the Passover Feast. It is sobering to surmise (yet impossible to know for sure) the emotions and sense of urgency He surely will feel today.

Today will be the last time He will be with His disciples until after His resurrection. I suspect for Peter and John and the others, there is excitement and joy in the air—a time almost jovial in nature. But as they prepare, I wonder what Jesus's thoughts are. This will be the last Passover feast that He would share with them. This is the time when He will wash their feet and teach them about servitude. This is the event where He will give them a new commandment. "Maundy" is a Latin word which means "commandment"—Jesus said to His disciples, "A new commandment I give unto you: that you love one another" (John 13:34).

Tomorrow will be the day that will change the whole world forever. Tomorrow, He will be alone. Tomorrow, that event for which He had come to earth will become reality. But tomorrow will come all too soon. Today, He still has His disciples with Him. Will He reflect on His past three years with them? Will He struggle with how to comfort them and prepare them for something they have no idea is just in front of them—and will need all the comfort possible? How does He express the depth of love He has for them—that love that will take Him to Golgotha? I wonder if He touches each of them and says, "I love you, Simon," "I love you, James," "I love

you, Phillip." How does He warn them, and teach them, and comfort them, and strengthen them, and . . .?

Indeed, as we try to visualize that scene in the Upper Room, our minds can become overloaded and our hearts humbled. The greatest event in all history is tomorrow! But Jesus's day will not wrap up with an emotional, energy-filled evening with His disciples in the Upper Room. No, the Garden of Gethsemane is still in front of Him with its agonizing and its inattentiveness and its solitude of prayer and the cutting off of the centurion's ear and the miracle of replacing it and then, finally, the betrayal by Judas.

I pray that today, you and I will pigeonhole away some time to meditate on what kind of a day Jesus is having. After all, one of His instructions on this day was: "This do in remembrance of Me."

Just look at what scriptures tells us about meditating:

- *__Meditate within your heart__ on your bed and be still* (Psalm 4:4b).
- *Let the words of my mouth and __the meditation of my heart__ be acceptable in Your sight, O Lord, my strength and my Redeemer* (Psalm 19:14).
- *I will __meditate on Your precepts,__ and contemplate Your ways* (Psalm 119:15).
- *I remember the days of old; __I meditate on all Your works__* (Psalm 143:5).

We will take our journey through Holy Week by each day asking the question: "What is today like for Jesus?" We will strive to go back two thousand years to those special eight days and bring them forward to today—as though they are happening now.

We will ask questions about Jesus and the disciples, about the crowds and Christ's enemies. We will examine the environment that made Jerusalem what it was during this time. We will strive to bring in the culture of the time and apply it to our study.

However, most of all, we want to wrap our minds around the events from a human perspective and from God's viewpoint. While that may seem to be a bit bold—looking at God's perspective—we actually have scripture to help us through it. We will strive to remind you of the human side of Jesus—the emotional side. How could it not have been a stressful time for Him?

We will fast-forward those two thousand years to today. As you go through your day, you will be able to think about what Jesus "is doing" today.

Finally, we will conclude each day with a personal devotion, making life application to what we studied. My prayer is that these eight days will forever carry new and deeper meaning for you as you journey through this life with Christ.

This book is the second in a series of books called ***Meditate on These Things.*** In Philippians 4:8, Paul says, *Finally, brethren, whatever things are true, whatever things are noble, whatever things are just, whatever things are pure, whatever things are lovely, whatever things are of good report, if there is any virtue and if there is anything praiseworthy—**meditate on these things.***

Chapter One

> "He who does not himself remember that God redeemed him from sin and death by the life and passion of Jesus of Nazareth ceases to be Christian."
>
> Paul Ramsey

For God so loved the world that He gave His only begotten Son, that whoever believes in Him should not perish but have everlasting life. For God did not send His Son into the world to condemn the world, but that the world through Him might be saved (**John 3:16-17**).

An Irrepressible Journey

As we begin this eight-day journey, I pray you will be taken deeper in your worship of Christ. I pray that this will become the most precious season of your year. If you can, do this devotional study early each day—before you get into your busy day. If you do, you will experience a more vibrant day.

Our goal is to bring time forward—more than two thousand years—for us to experience the events as they unfold. We want to be that proverbial "fly on the wall" that takes it all in. We want to be present on those dusty streets of Jerusalem, on the sleepy hills surrounding the city, in the crowded streets—bursting with people—shoulder to shoulder. We want to hear the sounds and smell the smells—to feel the electricity in the air. We could choose no more vital segment of time. For it was then and there that time and eternity collided and the greatest spiritual battle of all time played out in front of all who were there. Yet many did not even notice.

You may be doing other Passion Week studies as well. That is good. If so, this devotional will enhance and add depth to the thoughts and understanding you are already cultivating. However, it may be that this devotional is the totality of the time you will spend on the subject.

Regardless, please stop now and ask God to clear your mind of everything except this day—as it unfolded more than two thousand years ago.

"Jesus, please allow us in our hearts and minds to return to Jerusalem—as it was for You during this week so long ago. May we experience not only the excitement of the events that unfolded, but also help us understand how so much biblical prophecy was fulfilled—and how You revealed to us Your perfect plan of salvation. Amen."

The entrance of Jesus into Jerusalem on Palm Sunday was not the beginning of the end for Christ. It was not the culmination of a short but spectacular ministry and life. It was not the death of a great Prophet. It was not even the end of a good story—no, not at all.

Rather, the purpose of this journey was the purpose of His whole life. It was the reason for His very incarnation. Oh, it is true Jesus was and is the model for all mankind. It is true He taught many eternal lessons and He performed many miracles and wonders. It is true Jesus gave hope and joy and healing to many. It is also true He gave us guidance and instruction on how to please the Father. And especially, it is true Christ taught us the meaning of love and humility. There is so much for us to glean from the life of Jesus that we will never absorb it all—never.

But being a role model and doing incredible and miraculous things are not the reasons for His existence. Even His deep and meaningful teachings were not why He came into this world. Jesus, Himself, told us:

- ***I have come*** *that they may have life and that they may have it more abundantly* (John 10:10b).
- *For the **Son of Man has come** to seek and to save that which was lost* (Luke 19:10).
- And again, He said, *"**I have come** as a light into the world, that whoever believes in Me should not abide in darkness"* (John 12:46).
- *And whoever desires to be first among you, let him be your slave—just as the Son of Man did not **come** to be served, but to serve, and **to give His life** a ransom for many* (Matthew 20:28).

This journey to Jerusalem was birthed when man broke the perfect bond he had enjoyed with God. It was birthed when man became tarnished, flawed, and unrighteous by his disobedience in the Garden of Eden. Prior to the fruit and the serpent and his fall, man had an incredible life—he simply hung out with God. What a life! Walking through lush gardens, smelling the flowers, hand-in-hand with his wife and just listening to God. Oh, occasionally he had to take time away to name a few animals or birds. But that was quite fun actually. And that is just the way God wanted it.

But life changed drastically in a brief, yet eternal, moment. Sin had raised its ugly head, and the price for disobedience was to be very costly. God had said, *But of the tree of the knowledge of good and evil you shall not eat, for in the day that you eat of it **you shall surely die*** (Genesis 2:17).

To the woman, it included sorrow upon sorrow and pain in childbirth and the rule of a husband. *To the woman He said: "I will greatly multiply your sorrow and your conception; In pain you shall bring forth children; Your desire shall be for your husband, And he shall rule over you"* (Genesis 3:16).

For man, the ground would be cursed with thorns and thistles, and sweat from toiling would be a part of everyday life. And then for all mankind, death would not be escaped: *In the sweat of your face you shall eat bread till you return to the ground, for out of it you were taken; For dust you are and to dust you shall return* (Genesis 3:19).

But then, amidst the consequences, a plan that was *foreordained* **before the foundation of the** *world* (1 Peter 1:20a) was set in motion—unbeknown to man. It was a plan to restore fallen mankind—a plan so filled with love, compassion, and grace that once fulfilled, man struggled to believe it. Even today, many refuse to accept this gift—thus through their unbelief they refuse to be reconciled to God, instead facing an undeniable eternal separation from God Himself.

This journey of redemption began in earnest, however, in the region of Caesarea Philippi, when Christ was with His disciples and asked a poignant question: *But who do **you** say that I am?* (Matthew 16:15b).

There were various answers from the twelve—some recorded in scripture and surely some left unrecorded.

But it was Peter who answered Him correctly: *You are the Christ, the Son of the living God* (verse 16b). There it is! The Christ, the Son of the living God. You, Master, are the Christ (**Christos**–Greek), the anointed One, the Messiah (**Mashiyach**–Hebrew), the Deliverer. Jesus was the One the Hebrews had been waiting for over many centuries. He was the Promised One. He was the Messiah—the Savior of the world—of both the Jews and the Gentiles.

This was not just a test of theology for the twelve. Instead, it was a test of faith—a test of comprehension. Did they truly believe? Jesus wanted His disciples to know it and understand it. He wanted them to grasp the magnitude of it—that it was not a small thing Peter had just answered. It was huge. No, it was bigger than huge! It would rock the foundations of the world. This declaration that Jesus was the Promised One, the Messiah, the King of Kings was enormous in its revelation.

Here, for the first time, Jesus was emphatic that His disciples understand who He was. He was more than just a teacher or a miracle-worker or a prophet or a scriptural scholar. He was more than just the leader of twelve scruffy and disheveled men. He was not just the benevolent healer of blinded eyes or lame limbs. He was not just the feeder of the multitudes. No, maybe for the first time, Jesus wanted His disciples to know standing in front of them was the Savior of the world—the Promised One.

And this understanding and faith in Jesus must be grasped, for very soon their world would be rocked, their faith shaken, and their life would become a blur. The journey had started in earnest.

But this was not information to be shared with the world—not just yet. Jesus did not want the attention this revelation would create—not immediately anyway. He wanted no distractions. But He did want them to understand. Hence, He taught them. It was a crash course in Christian theology. And when He had finished, He set His attention toward Jerusalem—a place that would soon take on new meaning and hope—the Place of the Skull.

So, after He was finished saying to them:

- *My Father revealed it to you* (Matthew 16:17)
- *I will build My church* (Matthew 16:18)
- *The gates of Hell will not prevail* (Matthew 16:18).
- *I will give you the keys* (Matthew 16:19)
- *Whatever you bind on earth* (Matthew 16:19)

Matthew then records this: *Then He commanded His disciples that* **they should tell no one that He was Jesus the Christ.** *From that time Jesus began to show to His disciples that* **He must go to Jerusalem,** *and suffer many things from the elders and chief priests and scribes, and be killed, and be raised the third day* (Matthew 16:20-21).

Mark records Jesus saying, *Behold,* **we are going up to Jerusalem,** *and the Son of Man will be betrayed to the chief priests and to the scribes; and they will condemn Him to death and deliver Him to the Gentiles* (Mark 10:33).

But this trip to Jerusalem was not to be just another stop along the way. This was not to be a casual, "Hey, let's head up to Jerusalem tomorrow. I really like the place." Nor was this to be, "You know, we have not been to Jerusalem for a while. Let's head up there and see what's happening." No, this trip was to be different. It was not to be another crossing of the Sea of Galilee with its wind and its waves. It was not to be sitting on another hillside teaching and feeding the multitudes. This trip was not going to be looking for another Zacchaeus in a tree nor another woman at a well nor another demon-possessed man.

No, Luke makes it clear—this was a mission.

- *Now it came to pass, when the time had come for Him to be received up, that **He steadfastly set His face to go to Jerusalem*** (Luke 9:51).
- *But they did not receive Him, **because His face was [set] for the journey to Jerusalem*** (Luke 9:53).

Listen to those words again:

He steadfastly set His face...
His face was set for the journey...

Jesus had a mission, and He was not going to be deterred. What was that mission? Jesus tells us, *My food is to do the will of Him who sent Me, and to finish His work* (John 4:34). He will later acknowledge the fulfillment of the Father's will by whispering on the cross, *It is finished.* Jesus was focused and determined and resolute to go to Jerusalem to do what He had to do, to fulfill what He came to fulfill, to give what the Father desired to give to all mankind—the gift of salvation! And to Jerusalem it would be.

Later, as the journey to Jerusalem unfolded, Jesus gathered His twelve disciples to Himself and even more vividly tried to help them understand what was about to happen. *From that time Jesus began to show to His disciples that **He must go** to Jerusalem, and **suffer** many things from the elders and chief priests and scribes, and **be killed,** and be **raised** the third day* (Matthew 16:21).

A second time, in Galilee, Jesus speaks to them: *Now while they were staying in Galilee, Jesus said to them, "The Son of Man is about to be **betrayed** into the hands of men, and **they will kill Him,** and the third day He **will be raised up**"* (Matthew 17:22-23a).

And finally, a third time, Jesus explained to the twelve: *Now Jesus, going up to Jerusalem, took the twelve disciples aside on the road and said to them, "Behold, **we are going up to Jerusalem,** and the Son of Man **will be betrayed** to the chief priests and to the scribes; and **they will condemn** Him to death, **and deliver Him** to the Gentiles **to mock** and **to scourge** and **to crucify.** And the third day He will **rise again**"* (Matthew 20:17-19).

Unquestionably, Jesus was preparing His disciples for what was just ahead of them. Again, Luke tells us the story: *Then He took the twelve aside and said to them, "**Behold, we are going up to Jerusalem,** and all things that are written by the prophets concerning the Son of Man will be accomplished"* (Luke 18:31).

Even after arriving in Jerusalem—at the Passover Feast, just before prayer in the Garden—Jesus tried to assure His disciples. He wanted them to know that very soon their life with the Master would become their life with the Comforter: *And I will pray the Father, and he **shall give you another Comforter,** that he may abide with you for ever* (John 14:16, KJV). He wanted them to know that very soon the witnessing of miracles would be transformed into witnessing the greatest of miracle of all—a miracle of love and grace. And even after His resurrection, Jesus explained it would be their new "job" to tell the world of redemption completed: *But you shall receive power when the Holy Spirit has come upon you; and **you shall be witnesses** to Me in Jerusalem, and in all Judea and Samaria, and **to the end of the earth*** (Acts 1:8).

To the disciples, so little of what He was saying to them made sense. The twelve had grown comfortable following Jesus. They were captivated by the events that filled each day. The miracles, the crowds, and the attention that came their way because they followed Jesus captivated them. Little did they know soon their lives would unravel, their minds would race out of control, and their faith would be challenged. It would be eight days that would change the world.

And Jesus was headed to Jerusalem!

LIFE APPLICATION

And He said to them, "Why did you seek Me? Did you not know that I must be about My Father's business?" (Luke 2:49).

There is so much to be learned from Jesus as He prepared for "My Father's business." As you read this chapter, did you notice Jesus was not confused with His purpose in life? He knew exactly why He had come to this earth. He also was not distracted from His mission. The distance from Caesarea Philippi is almost 150 miles. There was plenty of time and plenty of distractions along that walk to Jerusalem. But Jesus stayed focused on His "mission."

Question: What is your purpose in life? Are you about your "Father's business," or do you allow the life of this world to confuse you and to distract you? Take some time today to identify what your purpose in life is.

You may already know that sin separates you from God, as told in Romans 5:12. It was the disobedience of Adam and Eve that caused them to be banned from the Garden of Eden and to bear the consequences of that sin.

Question: How often are you separated from God by your sin? Take time to identify the area(s) of your life where your actions or bitterness or anger or thoughts need to be cleansed. Then be steadfast in following Jesus!

Jesus asked His disciples this question: *Who do you say I am?* It is not a question just for the twelve. Every person must, in some form or fashion, confront the question and answer it in their heart and with their lips.

Question: Who is Jesus Christ to you? He wants to know. You need to know also. Search your heart and then make a list. Will you do that?

Satan desires to distract you. Please understand that! His whole purpose is to bury you under the silliness and insignificance of life. He wants you to be too busy for Jesus. He wants to draw your attention to anything but Jesus. Do not let him do it!

Chapter Two

> "Teach us, O Lord, the discipline of patience, for to wait is often harder than to work."
>
> Peter Marshall

So we do not lose heart. Though our outer self is wasting away, our inner self is being renewed day by day. For this light momentary affliction is preparing for us an eternal weight of glory beyond all comparison, as we look not to the things that are seen but to the things that are unseen. For the things that are seen are transient, but the things that are unseen are eternal (2 Corinthians 4:16-18, ESV).

Value in Waiting

Can you remember what it was like leading up to an important event in your life? Maybe it was your wedding day, the arrival of your first child, your first major vacation, your first day at college, Christmas morning for the kids, moving into your first new home, or maybe it was graduation day for you or a child or a grandchild. Whatever the special occasion, do you remember what the day before the special event was like—filled with the anticipation of tomorrow? Waiting and waiting and waiting.

Waiting is a strange phenomenon indeed. Anxiety pushes it way toward the brain while excitement climbs to a heightened state and anticipation simply explodes. The mind is filled with a million thoughts—all crashing together, striving to push their way to the forefront of your mind—but always seeming to fail—frantically mulling around inside of your being—disappearing for a while as attention is diverted, then reappearing—maybe a little more intense this time—somewhat better able to captivate your present thoughts.

Waiting . . . oh, how it can be so excruciating and yet so exciting. The anticipation seems to simply freeze time and wreak havoc with emotions. Waiting and waiting . . . just a little while longer—tomorrow is just around the corner. The last miles on the road back home seem to take forever, and yet a glance at the speedometer tells a different story. The last couple of hours on the flight to where family awaits feel like an eternity. Tomorrow is soon—but not nearly soon enough!

And it all happens as time seemingly slows to a crawl. Frequent glances at the clock do nothing to speed time up—in fact, they only seem to slow it even more. How frequent are the glances at the clock—even a pause—listening to make sure it is still ticking—all in anticipation of tomorrow? "I can't wait," or "Will this day never end," or "OMG, it is almost here!" are thoughts—among others—that ooze out of our minds and unto our lips. And yet, still we must wait—wait for tomorrow.

It's that day for Jesus.

It is the day before the first day—and Jesus must wait. It is the Sabbath—the day before the Triumphal Entry. The day before it all starts to happen—that fulfillment of prophecy and the anticipation of the Messiah.

But that day is tomorrow. Today is the Sabbath, the weekly day of rest—a day to slow down and worship God the Father—a day to put aside the world and its allure—a day to spend with the Lord.

Jesus's "normal" routine on the Sabbath was to go to the synagogue with His disciples, teach there, and then retreat somewhere to rest.

Though none of the gospels mention it, Jesus most certainly followed that Jewish custom and then likely journeyed back to the house of Lazarus to spend the day in rest from the work of the world, thus honoring the fourth commandment: *Remember the Sabbath day, to keep*

Palm Sunday to Resurrection Sunday

---

it holy. Six days you shall labor, and do all your work, but the seventh day is the Sabbath of the LORD your God (Exodus 20:8-10a).

There surely is a lot of excitement in the air on this Sabbath day. A quick look at the events of recent days tells us why. This was not just another time Jesus had come to town. No, Jesus has come back to town!

Earlier, He had raised Lazarus from the dead. The story is recorded in John, chapter 11. It is probably a familiar story to you. But not everyone was pleased with Jesus's miracle. John tells us, *Then, from that day on, **they plotted to put Him to death.** Therefore Jesus no longer walked openly among the Jews, but went from there into the country near the wilderness, to a city called Ephraim, and there remained with His disciples* (John 11:53-54).

Jesus and His followers had fled town—His life in jeopardy! They went to Ephraim, a town northwest of Jerusalem—near the wilderness—in the country. But they didn't stay there very long because Jesus knew His mission—He must be in Bethany just before the start—the start of His fulfillment of the Father's plan of redemption.

So, Bethany has to be at high-voltage as the word spreads concerning His return. Jesus has returned, and He is at the house of Lazarus. Jesus has come back to Bethany, but why? And they wonder, "Will we see Him in the synagogue?" "Surely we will! Yes, surely Jesus will be teaching in the synagogue today!" And the people are making plans to go early that they might not miss it!

While the town is electric, let us catch up with Jesus and His disciples on this day before the first day—of the eight days that changed the world.

I wonder what the walk to the synagogue is like for Jesus and the twelve as they traverse the dusty path to the Lord's house? There had been many of these days before. The Bible tells us of some of them:

- *Now He was teaching in one of **the synagogues on the Sabbath*** (Luke 13:10).
- *So He came to Nazareth, where He had been brought up. **And as His custom was,** He went into the synagogue on the Sabbath day, and stood up to read* (Luke 4:16).
- *Then He went down to Capernaum, a city of Galilee, and was **teaching them on the Sabbaths*** (Luke 4:31).

But today is not like prior Sabbaths. No, today is the last Sabbath the twelve will be with their Lord. It is the last Sabbath He will teach the scriptures to the people. It is His last Sabbath here on earth in His "unresurrected" body. Jesus knows it. Jesus understands the significance of it all. This is the fulfillment of thousands of years of anticipation. But for His disciples, it is simply another "normal" day with the Master.

Pause just now. Let us imagine this moment. Try to look at the face of Jesus as He walks along. I am not sure, but I think there is a little urgency to His step as He walks along with His head down and His followers lagging behind—chatting as they shuffle along the pathway. The chatter amongst the disciples is brisk and jovial—filled with questions and comments about where they were and what they did since they left Bethany. But Jesus seems preoccupied. Do you see that? Do you see how He seems resolute and focused on something other than the present moment?

But wait! Did you see Him just now raise His head and look out over the hills of Bethany? His spirit seems to immediately be lifted. What is He thinking? What caught His attention? It appears as though He is suddenly looking at the countryside. Is He admiring His creation? Yes, I think so! Does He see the flowers on the hillside, as they seem to lean their petals His way—acknowledging their Creator? Oh, I think so! And is Jesus—as His pace slows just a little—not delighting in His creation? Oh, again I think He is!

Look around—the sky appears brighter and the mountains grander. And aren't the birds chirping louder than usual—maybe even as an encouragement to their Maker? Wow, that's a thought: The Father using the created to bless and encourage their Creator! After all, here is the handiwork of Jesus—all the grandeur that He spoke into existence. And today is the last day He will have to enjoy them before the eight days begin.

Maybe Jesus is even remembering the scriptures as He recounts Moses's simplistic account of when Jesus created all of this: ***And God said ... and it was so ... And God made ... and God saw that it was good ... And God said "Let there be" ... and it was good*** (Genesis 1).

But as Moses seems to almost understate creation, God inserts verse 31 of that first chapter of Genesis: ***Then God saw everything that He had made, and indeed it was very good.*** "Oh, Moses, how I wish you could have been there when We spoke all of creation into being. It was glorious! Oh, how it blessed Us as We brought time into existence and as We watched the dust become living beings and the birds began to sing and on their wings—for the first time—soared to joyful heights! Oh, Moses, what a time it was as time began. Oh, how I love My creation! That is why I must walk through the next eight days—for My creation—My children—My disciples!"

Understand, I am not offering new words of Jesus here—but don't you think there are times that Jesus so desires for us to better understand the Father's plan of redemption? Don't you think He so wants His followers to clearly see how full of love these next eight days will be—yet so painful, so bloody, and so unjust? Isn't it reasonable to think that Jesus is just a little sad right now as He watches His followers stroll along—soon to be blindsided and confused by what is just in front of them? And don't you think Jesus would love to walk over to the twelve and assure them that all is still in the Father's hands? I do.

Is Jesus just now encouraged as He gazes at the splendor of His creation and breathes in the coolness of the morning? Or are things just getting too intense? And do the twelve know it? As they walk along, I wonder if the disciples sense a difference in Jesus—if indeed there is one?

Jesus is now in the synagogue, and all that has been supercharged and electric suddenly becomes silent. The crowds stop pushing and shoving for position—instead settling in to hear Jesus. They have filled the synagogue and are cramming the aisles and overflowing outside into the courtyard. Those that are arriving late are running to get there before Jesus begins to speak. Every window has five or six faces replacing the light of day. The doorways are blocked with people. And the children are quickly brought to a halt and quieted by a parent or an adult.

As the twelve are looking around the crowd, they realize something is different—but what is it? You can see their puzzled expressions as they try to sort it out. What is going on? Jesus taught in the synagogue on the Sabbath in Nazareth (Luke 4:16). But this is different. He taught in the synagogue on the Sabbath in Capernaum (Luke 4:31). But this is different. The crowds are different. The atmosphere is different. The excitement in the air is different. Jesus even taught in the synagogue on the Sabbath in Samaria, healing the woman with the spirit of infirmity (Luke 13:10-17). But today is so much different. What is it?

Maybe it is this Lazarus thing—people surprised we came back to Bethany. Or maybe it is the excitement of Passover. After all, tomorrow, we head into the city. Tomorrow, the Master will be in the Temple teaching. He has been warned not to go to Jerusalem, but He has been so set on it. Do you remember when He called us aside on the road and said, *Behold, we are going up to Jerusalem . . .?* (Mark 10:33a).

It is not embellishment to think there may be a sense of urgency in Christ on this day of waiting. After all, He was fully human as well as fully God. He had all the same emotions and feelings we have. He surely feels the urgency of time as He approaches this last week of His physical life. There will be many "last times" for Him in the coming days—the last time to enter the synagogue, the last time to pray with His disciples, the last time to assure them, the last time to dine with them, the last time to teach the multitudes, etc. Oh, Jesus is surely filled with anticipation and emotions. In fact, we will remind ourselves of this often as we walk this journey with Christ.

LIFE APPLICATION

But those who wait on the LORD shall renew their strength; They shall mount up with wings like eagles, They shall run and not be weary, They shall walk and not faint (Isaiah 40:31).

"It is not lost time to wait on God." – Hudson Taylor

Waiting on the Lord is not something in which most of us excel. But we are told often to do so:

- *Lead me in Your truth and teach me, For You are the God of my salvation; **On You I wait all the day** (Psalm 25:5).*
- ***Wait on the LORD**; Be of good courage, And He shall strengthen your heart; **Wait, I say, on the LORD!** (Psalm 27:14).*
- *So you, by the help of your God, return; Observe mercy and justice, **And wait on your God continually** (Hosea 12:6).*

So many times, when we pray, we want an immediate answer. It may be supplication for God to do something like healing or provisions. It may be looking for God's direction in a decision we are facing. It may be for wisdom in dealing with a family member, a friend, or a work situation.

But we rarely are comfortable when waiting for an answer. However, waiting on God is a lesson to be learned, and patience is a trait to desire. Waiting on the Lord takes the solution out of your hands and places it firmly in God's hands. It tests your faith, and when you see the result of waiting on Him, your faith grows.

Question: How often have you become impatient with God and acted before you received an answer? How often have you used your own strength or wisdom rather than waiting on God?

Please take a moment right now to reflect on this issue and then resolve to let God direct your path.

Often, the hardest challenge is waiting for the Holy Spirit to work in the heart of an unsaved child, parent, sibling, or close friend. A strong desire to see them receive the same life-changing salvation that we enjoy puts us on edge with a sense of urgency. We want it to happen now! And that is understandable. In fact, it is exactly how we should feel. However, what to do, what to say, and when to say or do it is another story.

Waiting on the Lord in situations like this is just plain difficult. But don't forget God's timing is always perfect. We need to "pray without ceasing" for our unsaved loved ones—and then be ready to be used by God when called upon.

Waiting on the Lord is a command directly from God's Word. However, there is a huge flag of caution waving all around: **Do not confuse waiting on the Lord with idleness.**

Jesus was not idle as He waited for His time to come. He continued on with the Father's work. On the way to Jerusalem—those 150 or so miles—there was much ministry that continued. Jesus continued to teach in the synagogue, give parables, instruct His followers, heal the afflicted, and on and on . . . In fact, His ministry increased during this time—probably because Jesus knew His appointed time was drawing near.

Please do not allow yourself to be spiritually paralyzed or wallow in a funk waiting and waiting for an answer from the Lord. You will dry up spiritually.

Question: What are you doing to continue on with the Master's work as you wait, pray, and watch for an answer to your prayer or supplication from God? Are you spiritually lethargic, sluggish, or even comatose as you wait?

Take the time to check your "patience meter." God will give you an answer if you listen, watch, and pray (and stay in His Word). He never forgets to give you one—in due season—and on time—His perfect time.

"Lord, help me to wait upon You with joy and patience as I continue on with Your work of loving those around us with Your love and telling the story of the lost lamb who was found—us." Amen.

Chapter Three

> "Ride on, ride on in majesty! In lowly pomp ride on to die; O Christ, thy triumphs now begin, O'er captive death and conquered sin."
>
> Henry Hart Milman

Rejoice greatly, O daughter of Zion! Shout, daughter of Jerusalem! See, your king comes to you; righteous and having salvation, gentle and riding on a donkey, on a colt, the foal of a donkey (Zechariah 9:9).

Passion Week – Day One
Palm Sunday

Today is the day that history will call Palm Sunday. It is the day of the "Triumphal Entry." It is the day of celebration for the King of Kings. Jesus's entry into Jerusalem this day will be filled with celebration—there will be a procession and excitement all around the Old City. Yet today will be so much more than that—and Jesus knows it.

It is now early morning, probably before sunrise. If you have ever been up before daylight, sitting on a hillside and praying, you may be able to relate in a small way to what Jesus is feeling as the quietness and the crispness of predawn awakens the senses. Nature begins to stir just before dawn—just before the sun gently squeezes out the darkness, stirring and illuminating creation. Being alone with nature early in the morning is an incredible experience. No wonder Jesus chose it as His time for prayer and supplication with the Father. There is a certain freshness and purity to it. The air is bold and invigorating. The smell of early morning is vibrant and inviting. Surely this is a very special morning for Jesus, a final time of solitude. Soon life will erupt into an avalanche of events—accelerating and intensifying as the days unfold. For Jesus, for His followers, for Jerusalem, and for the world—never again will things be the same. But just now, Jesus is praying.

Scripture does not tell us nor has history surmised what He is praying and for whom is He praying on this day. In fact, we are not even told that Jesus is praying on this morning—but surely, He is.

We know He is because scripture tells us it was His custom:

- He prayed while in Capernaum, near the start of His ministry and amidst much teaching and healing: *Now in the morning, having risen a long while before daylight, He went out and departed to a solitary place; and **there He prayed*** (Mark 1:35).
- He prayed prior to selecting and calling His disciples: *Now it came to pass in those days that He went out to the mountain to pray, and **continued all night in prayer** to God. And when it was day, He called His disciples to Himself; and from them He chose twelve whom He also named apostles* (Luke 6:12-13).
- His praying even captivated His disciples so that they wanted the same power of prayer: *Now it came to pass, **as He was praying** in a certain place, when He ceased, that one of His disciples said to Him, "Lord, teach us to pray, as John also taught his disciples"* (Luke 11:1).
- He was praying after feeding the five thousand: *So they all ate and were filled, and twelve baskets of the leftover fragments were taken up by them. And it happened, **as He was alone***

praying, *that His disciples joined Him, and He asked them, saying, "Who do the crowds say that I am?"* (Luke 9:17-18).

Kneeling in prayer is the humble Jesus. It is not the proclaiming Jesus or the healing Jesus or the Shepherd Jesus—it is the humble Jesus. You can see it in His countenance. You can see it in His spirit and His face. Jesus is kneeling before the Father with eight days of testing and torment and trials clearly in His sight.

He knew this time was coming. All He ever did and said in past days and past years were preparation for this time—preparing His disciples, preparing His followers, preparing the people, preparing the world. But now the preparation is over. The teaching is almost over. Oh, there will be a last flood of parables in the coming days, but now it is time—time to fulfill what the prophets of old foretold. No more waiting. Today is day one, and it all begins now. And for Jesus (the man), it brings Him to His knees.

It is almost impossible to describe the feeling in the air. Tension is off the charts, and yet it is tempered with a consuming peace. It is electricity tamed. It is fear harnessed. It is apprehension calmed. It is anxiety soothed. It is all that is unsettling—settled. All the extremes of calamity and serenity are mingled and meshed and then taken captive by an absolute faith in the Father. One can almost hear Jesus softly singing the words of a song to be written centuries later:

Peace, peace, wonderful peace,
Coming down from the Father above.
Sweep over my spirit forever, I pray
In fathomless Billows of love!
— Warren D. Cornell and William G. Cooper, 1889

Jesus sits at peace with the will of the Father directly in front of Him—to be fulfilled a few days from now when He will proclaim to the world, *It is finished!* (John 19:30b).

And Jesus is praying. What is on the Savior's mind just now can only be guessing. But let us guess anyway.

Surely, His disciples are on His mind. Does the Savior have a special prayer for Judas? Judas only has a few more days before he will take his own life in despair. But Judas does not even know it. Oh, how it must sadden Christ as He prays for Judas. And is that Thomas's name we just heard? I think it was—Thomas, the one Jesus will invite to touch His riven side. Certainly "the Doubter" will need a new measure of faith, as the events ahead will raise more questions than provide answers for him and the others. I am quite sure He is praying for Thomas.

And what about John and Peter? They will become the leaders of the remaining eleven soon. "Oh, my beloved John, I pray for strength for you!" One by one, you can see their names form on His lips as Jesus lifts them up to the Father. Oh, how Jesus loves the twelve! As He prays for them, can you not almost see His face beam as He brings them to mind?

Could it be that Jesus is praying for you and me this morning as well? Do His thoughts race through time—in God speed—bringing to mind each of us? It is a noble thought—I rather like it—my name on Jesus's lips!

I am confident Jesus is praying for Himself this morning also. The magnitude of what is just in front of Him is impossible for us to comprehend. Tell me, how do we wrap our hearts and minds around what is in front of Jesus—the entry into the city today, the moneychangers in the temple, the teaching that yet must be done, the arrangements and the celebration of the Passover feast? It is a strange thought, but Jesus needs prayer today. The human Jesus faced temptation and anxiety—just as we do. In anguish, later in the week, He will cry out to the Father, *Father, if it is Your will,* **take this cup away from Me;** *nevertheless not My will, but Yours, be done* (Luke 22:42).

The thought that Jesus would be praying for His disciples and believers (you and me) and Himself is not just speculation. For in John, chapter 17, Jesus does just that. We will look at that in a later chapter.

Bethany, where Jesus is praying, is but a scant two miles southeast of Jerusalem. Though wrapped in a valley and over the hills and out of sight of Jerusalem, in the early morning hours, it is probable that Jesus is listening as the sounds of Jerusalem wind their way through the darkness to this place of prayer. And with each sound, Jesus visualizes people. And He prays.

He sees the thief and the thug and the other criminals doing their cowardly deeds under the cloak of darkness. And Jesus prays. He hears the people stirring in their dwellings, and He prays.

Palm Sunday to Resurrection Sunday

Jesus hears the sounds of the moneychangers setting up shop in the temple. He hears the excitement of those hoping to catch a glimpse of Him in Jerusalem. They heard He was coming for Passover. Jesus sees the faces of those He had healed in Galilee—those who are in Jerusalem for the Passover Feast. He listens as the Scribes and Pharisees grapple with what to do with Him. And Jesus prays for them all.

Could it also be that Jesus is thinking about the two who will be by His side in a few days—also to be crucified? Could it be He is thinking back to another time in Samaria, a time when He was teaching about the Kingdom of God and one being taken and one left behind? Soon one thief will be taken to Paradise and the other sent to eternal torment. Does Jesus pray for those criminals? Oh, surely, He does!

Finally, the faces of all who will line the street along His journey to Calvary are passing before Him. The Romans, the Galileans, the barterers and the bankers—His followers and His adversaries all come to mind. Then there is Simon, the Cyrenian—the one who will carry the cross—and, finally, Joseph from Arimathea, in whose tomb Jesus's body will be laid. And Jesus prays! Later on, Jesus will look over the city and weep for it. But just now, He surely is listening to the sounds of the city, and He is praying.

Let's you and I stop just now and pray for our own day—just as Jesus did so long ago.

"Come, hurry, please! Let us not lag behind!" The voices in the neighborhood are bursting with anxiety as Jesus begins the trek to Jerusalem. The pace is brisk, and the dust from sandaled feet is swirling around Jesus and His followers as they set out along the ridge of the Mount of Olives. There is excitement in the air—the scene like a hundred bees each swarming to the same fragrant flower, drawn by its beauty and gentleness.

The word is rapidly spreading that Jesus is heading for Jerusalem. Though it is still early, Bethany is rapidly coming to life. You can hear their voices and calls: "Jesus of Nazareth is here!" "Have you heard?"

"Have you seen Him?" "Jesus is on the way—on the road to Jerusalem." "I did not think He would come back, but I saw Him pass by just a moment ago." "No, no, He went that way. They are all just around the bend." "Hurry, let us try to catch up!" "Jesus of Nazareth is here!" "Jesus is here!" "Look, look, over there—Jesus is here!"

People are coming from all directions, scurrying to catch the procession, running and even shoving their way to get a glimpse of the "miracle worker"—the Man of Galilee. The once silent streets that just moments ago yielded only the sweet sound of the wind and the chirping of birds are now bursting with the sounds of people—people energized by Jesus.

With every step, the crowd swells. At the start, in Bethany, there were but Jesus, the twelve, and a handful of disciples. But now, the followers have grown into a crowd, and later on, it will become "the multitudes."

Winding over the hills, down through the narrow slopes and along the rim of the valley floor, Jesus continues the journey—the journey to Jerusalem—the journey that began in Caesarea Philippi. The sound of the crowd is expanding as song begins to mix with cheers and then mingles with the shouts of the people and the screams and the squeals of children.

No rock star or movie star or star athlete or political leader has ever stirred a crowd like the presence of Jesus. None like this crowd—on this morning.

Stop, just a moment, and look around at the crowds that are gathering. Do you see those in the shadows and those peering from behind the trees and buildings? Their curious looks tell a plethora of stories. Some say they had heard of Jesus but never encountered Him—not even from afar. Who is He anyway? Did He really give blind people their sight? How did He do that? And what about the lame? Did He really heal their legs so they could walk again? If so, what manner of man is this?

Others are hearing the name of Jesus for the first time and are struggling to understand the uproar. They watch the excitement all around them and eagerly stretch their necks to catch a glimpse of this Man from Galilee.

And over there is one who had sat on the hillsides of Galilee some time ago, laughing and mocking as Jesus taught the multitudes. But now, he is quiet, taking it all in, standing in the shadows. Could it be he is starting to believe? Maybe he continued to mock and harass Jesus in other places until one day he saw Jesus heal a lame man and then witnessed Jesus casting out a demon, and then he saw the gentleness as the Lord bent down and picked up a little child and placed him on His lap.

Now, he no longer mocks; he is just lingering in the shadows, watching. Could it be this man will still be following Jesus later as He is on the Via Delarosa and then at the hill Golgotha? And do you think Jesus sees him just now standing in the shadows as He and the crowds pass by?

Jerusalem is drawing nearer, and the crowds are swelling as they reach the road that will lead them down through the Kidron Valley and up to the gates of the city.

Suddenly, as He comes to Mount Olivet, Jesus pauses, turns, and speaks to two of His disciples. They nod their heads, turn toward the village opposite them, and begin to hurry as Jesus could be heard calling behind them, *If anyone says to you, why...Say because the Lord...* (Luke 19:31). The words struggle to catch up to the two as they hurry away. What did Jesus say to them, and why are they going into the village? Probably for supplies!

The crowds are growing as everyone has stopped moving along because Jesus has stopped. People are mingling around, and the pause has allowed family members and friends to find each other and to discuss what they are witnessing. Arms are waving as people are calling out to each other, desiring to share this phenomenon with loved ones or friends. People are resting as best they can, sitting on a rock or leaning against a tree or propped up by a wall, all the while diligently watching to make sure the Teacher does not leave. They remain ready to spring to their feet if Jesus and the crowd begin to move again. But just now, they are resting and watching the activity around them, and keeping an eye on Jesus.

Even though the procession has stopped, the electricity in the air has not subsided. It has only become more centralized. The crowd is stirring within itself, but not dispersing at all. Like an organizing tornado, the crowd becomes more tightly wrapped together, squeezed and pulled together—all drawn by this man Jesus.

The two disciples are hurrying to carry out the Master's instructions. Neither the Bible nor tradition names the disciples—it doesn't matter. Their destination is the village of Bethphage, near Mount Olivet. According to Jewish law, people were allowed to travel but two thousand cubits (about one thousand meters) on the Sabbath. Bethphage was at the outer limits from the Eastern Gate of Jerusalem. Hence, though clearly but a "passing through place" on the road from Jericho to Jerusalem, Bethphage was a place to spend the night.

Like most small villages, not much attention is given to it nor is attention wanted. The folks are generally quiet and unassuming, with their favorite pastime mostly sitting around watching people as their journey takes them through the village, down the Kidron Valley and up through the Eastern Gate of the city. There are some interesting characters here, to be sure, but most are simply plain folk and hardly noteworthy.

The two are hurrying toward the village, their eyes looking intently from side to side—searching for something. As they walk along, it becomes apparent that their Master's instructions were to go somewhere and find something. What might it be? It surely does not look like a supply run now!

The village sign is but a few strides behind them when the disciples stop suddenly, the strides of both halted in midair. Their eyes are looking to the right, focused on a colt nearby tethered beside his mother. One of them spots the colt and is pointing in its direction. The other nods in agreement and softly but excitedly exclaims, "Yes, that is the one!" Together, they approach the colt and loose its rope.

The disciples are so focused on their mission that they do not notice the many eyes watching them as they head toward the colt and its mother. But unmistakably, the men sitting along the wayside have suddenly begun to sit more uprightly, watching every movement of the disciples. Their demeanor is bordering on menacing—each of them appear ready to pounce in an instant, should those two strangers desire to steal their friend's animals. Suddenly, the sleepy little village and its occupants feel anything but sluggish and docile.

Almost in an orchestrated manner, some of those sitting under the trees and hanging around the structures begin to stir, while others stand up, and still others start walking toward Jesus's disciples. The tension is building like an afternoon thunderstorm—heading for certain conflict. And the disciples can feel it.

The looks on their faces expose the thoughts racing through their minds: *What do we do now? The Lord had said, "If anyone asks you." He did not say, "Ask to borrow the colt." He said, "If anyone asks you, say..."*

Well, no one asked, and now the situation is failing fast as the disciples stand motionless, trying to figure out what to do next.

Then suddenly, the silence is broken by the stern words of the animal's owner as he approaches the disciples: *Why are you loosing the colt?* (Luke 19:33). The men nearby, all in action-ready mode, cock their heads to hear the answer. It had better be the right one!

The answer comes from the mouth of Jesus—now being repeated exactly by the two disciples: *Because the Lord has need of it* (Luke 19:31).

Immediately, a sleepy, docile village returns. The calming of the Sea of Galilee was no more dramatic. The freeing of the demon-possessed man was no swifter. In an instant—with seven words—anger evaporates, tension vanishes, and no further discussion or explanation is required. There are no questions. There is no explanation. There is no bartering or negotiating. None is needed—"because the Lord has need of it!"

As the drama unfolds, we need to be reminded we are witnessing the words of the prophets of old being fulfilled: *Rejoice greatly, O daughter of Zion! Shout, daughter of Jerusalem! See, your king comes to you; righteous and having salvation, gentle and **riding on a donkey, on a colt, the foal of a donkey*** (Zechariah 9:9).

As the disciples turn and head away, there is silence all around. Not a word is spoken, not a muscle moves until the little colt is but a speck in the distance. Truly, what manner of man is this Jesus? It is several minutes before normalcy begins to return—but it really does not return completely—at least not for the rest of this day.

As the owner watches his prize colt disappear, you can see his mind racing through what is happening: *Two strangers just took my colt without paying for it, and I am fine with it! Wow! The Lord had need of **my** colt!*

Surely, later that day, the owner will hear why the Lord needs his colt. Surely, the roar of the multitudes and the disruption of the Triumphal Entry will be felt in the little village close by.

And suddenly, there is one noteworthy resident in Bethphage.

Jesus is in the midst of the people as He awaits the disciples' return from the nearby village. Jesus always seemed to be amongst the people—and He was always moved with compassion for them. We learned that from Matthew, when Jesus was in Galilee, *But when He saw the multitudes,* **_He was moved with compassion for them,_** *because they were weary and scattered, like sheep having no shepherd* (Matthew 9:36).

But Jesus is not idle—He is teaching—it is His custom:

- *Then He arose from there and came to the region of Judea by the other side of the Jordan. And multitudes gathered to Him again,* **_and as He was accustomed, He taught them again_** (Mark 10:1).
- *But when the multitudes knew it, they followed Him; and* **_He received them and spoke to them about the kingdom of God,_** *and healed those who had need of healing* (Luke 9:11).

Many are pushing their way through the crowd, reaching out to touch Jesus. There are a few frustrated glances—but for the most part, people are more focused on Jesus than those around them. Some stand in awe, unable to move or speak—captivated by the presence of Jesus. Others are hyper and flitting about, not sure where to go or what to do, but quite determined to do it anyway.

The throngs are here to see Jesus. Just prior, the number of followers was much smaller—but now they are the multitudes. Were it not so exciting, the sheer volume of people crammed near the descent from the Mount of Olives to the Kidron Valley below would feel threatening. But just now it does not feel that way at all.

Then suddenly, Zechariah 9:9 begins to unfold. The colt, with his mother, has arrived. And as the disciples draw near to Jesus, cloths are being placed on the colt and Jesus is being lifted up—now He is sitting head and shoulders above the crowd.

And the multitude of people—as if on cue from the prophet—bring to life the words foretold over five hundred years earlier: *Rejoice greatly, O daughter of Zion! Shout, daughter of Jerusalem! See, your king comes to you; righteous and having salvation, gentle and **riding on a donkey, on a colt, the foal of a donkey*** (Zechariah 9:9).

The significance of this moment cannot be overstated. In fact, efforts throughout history to explain its magnitude will be woefully feeble. Descriptions of the adoration and worship that is unfolding barely tell the story. But Jesus is not going to allow history to be robbed of this moment's power and glory. For now, His time has arrived.

Before this time, Jesus had often exhorted His followers to not tell what they had just seen. He told His mother, *My hour has not yet come* (John 2:4). He charged Jarius and his wife to tell no one what had happened. He commanded the deaf man to tell no one. He commanded His disciples to tell no one He was the Christ.

Even when His brothers exhorted Him to go to the Feast of Tabernacles that He might show Himself to the world, Jesus replied, "My time has not yet come."

The Hebrew people and the world had waited more than 1,400 years since Moses first foretold of the Messiah in Genesis 3:15. Down through the ages, more than 125 prophecies in over three thousand scriptures had spoken of the Messiah. And the world waited. And the Hebrew people waited.

The wait is over!

The colt begins to slowly move toward the descent just ahead, and as the great crowd moves along, palm branches are being cut, then waved and even thrown on the path in front of Jesus—a symbol of victory, triumph, peace, and eternal life.

Some of the followers are ripping off their garments and throwing them in His path as the colt begins to move forward and the followers, both behind and in front of Jesus, begin to cry out, *Hosanna to the Son of David! Blessed is He who comes in the name of the Lord! Peace in heaven and glory in the highest! Hosanna, Hosanna in the highest!* (Psalm 118:26), which means "O save!" or "Deliver us!"

The energy of the multitudes is rapidly expanding, and the noise is getting louder by the second. More people are cutting their own palm branches and running and spreading them on the road in front of the colt as it slowly makes its way down the steep hill. The people are swirling around the Master, and the glow on their faces scream out pure joy. "Hosanna, Hosanna in the highest!"

Jesus is doing nothing to incite the crowd. But then neither is He trying to quiet them. He does not have the politician's wave or the haughty celebrity's gloat. He is simply sitting there, taking it all in, knowing that the words of the prophet Zechariah are being fulfilled at this very moment. The road that leads down to the valley floor is a steep descent. Though infrequent, a heavy rain will make the usually pleasant trek a challenging obstacle. Even though well-traveled, this segment of road remains one of the most beautiful and serene stretches of road along any route of those leading up to Jerusalem.

Trees line the way almost as a memorial to the burial grounds of the countless forefathers who have been laid to rest on the hillsides of the Mount of Olives—just to the left. Though a busy road, it is more of a dusty path than a conditioned road. At the bottom is the olive garden they call Gethsemane, and if you are making the journey in the early morning—before the merchants appear—it is a pleasant trek indeed.

This path will become known as "Palm Sunday Way," and thousands will travel down the six-tenths of a mile descent during annual pilgrimages.

But trees and tombstones and treacherous roads take no residence in anyone's mind today. Oh no! Jesus is here, and He is coming to Jerusalem. Jesus is here! The crowd is no longer a crowd—it is growing into a multitude—make that a very great multitude. In fact, both Matthew and Luke tell us so:

- *And **a very great multitude** spread their clothes on the road; others cut down branches from the trees and spread them on the road* (Matthew 21:8).
- ***The whole multitude of the disciples began to rejoice*** (Luke 19:37b).

The slope is steep, but the followers are not deterred. Their energy is not waning, and their enthusiasm is not diminishing; in the distance, you can see people running out of the gates of the city. They have indeed heard the roar and are joining in the celebration. All of heaven seems to be joining in as the people cry out in worship to the King of Kings. The disciples continue to run and shout and sing and cheer all around.

But Luke tells us not everyone is happy. In the crowd are the ever-present Pharisees—the self-declared religious leaders. And as always, wherever Jesus went, the Pharisees followed—not to glean from His wisdom—but to gather accusations against Him. Just now, the size, enthusiasm, worship, and adoration of the crowd was of deep concern to them, and they exhorted Jesus to calm the people: *Teacher, rebuke Your disciples* (Luke 19:39).

The pleas are repeated. Sadly, the Pharisees are so entwined in their own purposes that they fail to understand the magnitude of what is happening. If anyone, as religious scholars, they should understand the meaning of the scene before them. But they do not, and hence, it is a somewhat strange scene.

Their challenge to the Messiah is like the sparrow taunting the eagle. It is the minnow slamming into the side of the orca. It is the squirrel chirping at the grizzly. It is anger and hate mixed with fear. Their shouts are forcefully mixed with apprehension, and they plow forward with a demand they know to be wrong—but they do it anyway. They had heard of the great works of this man. Some had even seen. But they continue to call out to Jesus—telling Him to stop the celebration of the arrival of the Promised Messiah.

Jesus listens, allowing the Pharisees to burn off some of the hate and anger they feel toward Him. He has the look of a parent watching His child badly misbehaving.

In due time, Jesus responds to the religious leaders with one of theology's most concrete truths about Himself: *I tell you that if these should keep silent, the stones would immediately cry out* (Luke 19:40b). In one little sentence, Jesus proclaims that all of nature acknowledges that He is their Creator. God does not need man to be praised! All of creation cries out the glory of God every day. And Jesus is saying to the Pharisees, "I will be praised, I will be worshipped, I will be glorified."

King David said just that: *The heavens declare the glory of God; And the firmament shows His handiwork. Day unto day utters speech, and night unto night reveals knowledge. There is no speech nor language where their voice is not heard* (Psalm 19:1-3).

The squirrel quits chirping at the grizzly.

As Jerusalem is getting closer, Jesus sees the city and weeps over it. *Now as He drew near, He saw the city and wept over it* (Luke 19:41). It would be permissible to surmise what this moment was like in real life and real time—this moment of extreme emotion for Jesus, this moment that brought Him to weep.

We could place a length of time on it. We could make it a few minutes or a few seconds in duration. We could determine whether it was a dramatic moment, deciding that He shouted out the words and the great multitudes paused their rejoicing to listen to the words of Jesus.

Or maybe we would determine that only those close by heard His words, for maybe He spoke in a small voice. We could paint a word picture of what we determined were the thoughts of Jesus that caused this emotion from Him. We may—even as many do—focus on the people around Him, believing He was thinking about how He would die for them soon, and that brought Him to tears.

But to do so would be pointless. Jesus has a history with Jerusalem:

- He was born just five miles away in Bethlehem.
- His parents took Him there annually for Passover.
- He lingered there as a boy of twelve, in the Temple.
- He was tempted by Satan there.
- He taught there frequently.
- He was protective of the Temple, cleansing it twice.
- He would soon hang and die just outside its gates.

But Jerusalem was not just a place of many memories for Jesus. No, no, Jerusalem is so much more. It is:

- Moriah – The-Lord-Will-Provide (Genesis 22:14).
- Mountain of the Lord (Isaiah 2:3).
- City of righteousness, the faithful city (Isaiah 21:6).
- Holy place of the tabernacle of the Most High (Psalm 46:4)
- City of Truth (Zechariah 8:3).
- The city that shall be called: THE LORD IS THERE (Ezekiel 48:35).
- Holy City (Matthew 4:5).

For God Jesus, this place is special. He was there when at this place:

- Abraham offered his son Isaac to the Lord, as commanded.
- Melchizedek ruled and the city was called Salem.
- King David established it as the capital of a united Israel.
- The temple was built by Solomon.
- Four hundred years earlier, Artaxerxes commanded to rebuild Temple, starting the clock on the great prophecy in Daniel 9:25 — prophecy of the Messiah.
- Hezekiah built his tunnels.
- Nebuchadnezzar destroyed the Temple and city and exiled the Jews to Babylon.
- Ezra rebuilt the Temple and the walls of the city.
- Ptolemy captured the city.
- King Herod captured the city and began to rebuild the Temple.

There is no question, Jesus is thinking about His beloved Jerusalem. But just now, He is not captivated by the vast history and significance of this great city.

To understand this passage, we should examine the meaning of at least two of the words of this passage (Luke 19:41) — the words *saw* and *wept.* To do so, we have looked at the meaning of those words in the Greek as taken from Strong's Concordance.

In the KJV, the word used is *beheld* rather than "saw" — they mean the same. In some cases, this word "beheld" can mean an intense or strong emotional observation — almost as if the observer is in awe. It can mean to gaze with wonder. It would be appropriate for Jesus to gaze over the city in awe — but not here.

Jesus is not gazing in wonder at Jerusalem. Rather, here the word means "to express merely a mechanical, passive or casual vision" (see Strong's #G1492 & #G3700 for Greek meaning). Jesus saw Jerusalem. The city was in His vision. It did not captivate Him as one might be captivated when viewing the Grand Canyon. It simply appeared in His vision, and He became aware of it.

The word *wept* here is not "to sob softly." It is not to cry discreetly with a few whimpers. It is not a few tears that gather in the corner of the eye before one composes himself again. No, here, the word is "klaio" (see Strong's #G2799 for Greek meaning) which means "to wail aloud."

Jesus began wailing aloud as He caught a glimpse of Jerusalem. Why? If it was not caused by recalling all the grandeur of the city—if it was not due to recalling all the personal memories of the city—then what was it?

Well, let us look at what we are told by Luke:

> *Now as He drew near, He saw the city and wept over it, saying, "If you had known, even you, especially in this your day, the things that make for your peace! But now they are hidden from your eyes. For days will come upon you when your enemies will build an embankment around you, surround you and close you in on every side, and level you, and your children within you, to the ground; and they will not leave in you one stone upon another, because you did not know the time of your visitation."*
>
> – Luke 19:41-44

As we examine this scripture, we get a glimpse at what Jesus is thinking and feeling just now. Jerusalem's day was at hand—the day when it would welcome in the King of Kings—the day that she would host the Prince of Peace. But Jerusalem would not recognize its King. And it caused Him to wail aloud, *"If you had known,"* (Luke 19:42) and *"But now they are hidden from your eyes."* (Luke 19:42).

It would be only a short time and Jerusalem would pay a heavy price for its rejection of Jesus—its destruction in 70 AD. And that reality caused Jesus to wail aloud.

However, Jesus's relationship with Jerusalem does not end with its destruction. Jesus and Jerusalem still have a close relationship, for this place will one day become Mount Zion, the city of the living God, as described in Hebrews 12:22-24a: *But you have come to Mount Zion and to the city of the living God, the heavenly Jerusalem, to an innumerable company of angels, to the general assembly and church of the firstborn who are registered in heaven, to God the Judge of all, to the spirits of just men made perfect, to Jesus the Mediator of the new covenant.*

Jesus will indeed be Lord of Lords in His New Jerusalem!

The multitude has mostly dispersed, the colt has been returned to its owner, Jerusalem is still abuzz with Passover, but the city is no longer frantic. And Jesus is headed to the Temple.

Just a few moments ago, the city was moved as Jesus and the multitudes came through the Eastern Gate into Jerusalem. The procession took quite a while to clear the city walls, and many around inquired about this man—who was He, and what was going on? They could sense the excitement, and their ears had been tracking the constant cheering as the procession had wound its way down from the Mount of Olives, across the Kidron Valley, and up into the city with its shouts of "Hosanna, Hosanna!" Why? *This is Jesus, the prophet from Nazareth of Galilee* (Matthew 21:11b).

At this point, do you feel the urge to scream, "What? The prophet? Are you kidding me? No, no, no! This is God, the Savior, the Messiah. This is not 'the prophet' from Nazareth"? But Jesus did not react, nor did He correct those around Him. Likewise, O Lord, let my silence be my wisdom.

Jesus is now at the Temple. Most of the people are gone, their emotions shot, their energy evaporated, their strength spent. Many went back to their homes in the city and the surrounding villages. Some dispersed to their lodging, be it hut or tent. Some went to see friends or relatives to share the news of the event that had just transpired. But most just disappeared—back into the day.

The twelve are still here, and there are a few curious others milling about and gawking at Jesus, but mostly it is how it usually is at the Temple during Passover.

Jesus is in the Temple now, looking around. But He is more than just casually looking around. Mark pens it this way: *So when He had looked around at all things* (Mark 11:11b). This was not Jesus sticking His head in the door to say, "Hi," to the workers in the Temple. No, not at all! This was an inspection. Jesus is inspecting the entire Temple—all things! All the things in the Temple and all the things happening in and around the Temple do not escape the eye of Jesus.

There is scarcely any conversation between Jesus and the twelve, or Jesus and anyone actually. The twelve watch, moving about, occasionally talking to others in the Temple, but not to Jesus.

The minutes are turning into hours as Jesus files mental note after mental note during His walk through the Temple. It is hard to determine His thoughts. There appears to be an occasional twinkle of pleasure in His eye, but mostly the expressions shift between sadness, frustration, and anger—sometimes a mixture of each. What is Jesus thinking? It would be grossly futile to even guess His thoughts at this time. So, we will not.

The walk back to Bethany is void of all the energy and adrenalin of this morning. Mostly, Jesus and the twelve slowly trudge along the two-mile trip painstakingly and silently. The climb up the hill to the Mount of Olives is particularly difficult. A brief pause at the top of the hill provides a small relief to weary legs and feet. The pause also provides a moment for the thoughts and emotions of earlier to return as they turn and look back at the city. Some sigh in wonder as they recount the crazy day. Some laugh in satisfaction, almost like the pride of accomplishment after a hard-fought contest. Others mumble, still in amazement. But

Palm Sunday to Resurrection Sunday

Jesus just stands there and looks at Jerusalem, before moving on. The full significance of this is lost on all of them—but not Jesus.

As they settle in the house in Bethany, they help Him take off His sandals. There is a restless weariness in the house, which will be home base for Jesus most of this Passover week. Jesus is physically exhausted, and those ministering to Him are working overtime to care for His needs.

And slowly the sun sets on Day One.

LIFE APPLICATION

Watch therefore, and pray always that you may be counted worthy to escape all these things that will come to pass, and to stand before the Son of Man (Luke 21:36).

If you have been a Christian for even a short amount of time, you probably have heard and believe in the importance and the power of prayer. You have heard it in teachings, you have read of its power in Scripture, and hopefully you have experienced the power of your own prayers.

Yet the place of prayer is home to more spiritual battles than any other area of our Christian life—maybe all combined. It is bloody, it is brutal, and it is constant. In fact, a recent movie called the place of prayer "the War Room" and well it is. However, it also can just as aptly be called the Victory Room. For in prayer we are protected when tempted (Luke 22:40), we are given strength that we do not lose heart (Luke 18:1), and we can have a real impact (James 5:16).

Question: How consistent is your prayer time? Is your prayer life strong or weak? What do you plan to do to make it better? If you need help in this area, get with a prayer warrior you know or your pastor. They can help you.

Many times, in the journey described today, people asked a simple question: "Who is this Man?" It is a fair question. By the time Jesus reached Jerusalem, His reputation and notoriety had gone off the charts. He was the most discussed and debated person anywhere. Who is this Man?

Question: How do you answer that question today? What do you say when your family or friends think He is not God? Your answer is everything. It is important for you to consider what others say about Jesus and equip yourself with a strong biblical response.

Before the Triumphal Entry, Jesus did not need to send His disciples to get the colt. He could have had the colt there as needed for the Triumphal Entry. But God usually chooses man to accomplish His purposes.

Question: What is the Lord asking you to do? Today? Right now? Is He asking you to do it by faith? Or is He asking you to do it by obedience? Take the time today to ask Him how He wants to use you for His purposes.

Chapter Four

> "Our Lord never condemned the fig tree because it brought forth so much fruit that some fell to the ground and spoiled. He only cursed it when it was barren."
>
> Edwin Louis Cole

When He came to it, He found nothing but leaves, for it was not the season for figs. In response Jesus said to it, "Let no one eat fruit from you ever again." And His disciples heard it (Mark 11:12-14).

Passion Week – Day Two
Fig Monday

Morning has come early—or so it seems to Jesus's disciples and the twelve. To say the events of yesterday had taken a physical toll on most of them would be somewhat of an understatement. A few had been so exhausted, sleep was unavoidable—coming almost before their head found a resting place. For others, there was still too much adrenalin to slumber. Frequent tossing and turning was their companion for several hours, and now the short night's rest is felt throughout their bodies. As usual, Jesus is alone on the hillside.

Palm Sunday to Resurrection Sunday

As people begin to rise and make their assorted efforts to "get it together," pockets of conversation begin to crop up. Mostly, the talk is about yesterday: "Can you believe that?" "I couldn't believe how fast people appeared! They were coming from everywhere!" "I was a little scared actually. Everyone was rushing toward Jesus and us." "Could you believe the noise? It was so loud, people from Jerusalem heard the noise and started running out to see what was happening!" "Yes, and then they started to join in worshipping Jesus." "Did you see Jesus's face when they shouted, 'Hosanna, Hosanna!'? You could tell He liked it. He just seemed to be taking it all in." On and on, the uniqueness and the spontaneity of yesterday are occupying their minds and conversation.

Eventually, the conversation slowly turns to today—wondering what it will bring. "We will be going back into the city again today." "I wonder where we will celebrate the Feast this year?" "Do you think today will be anything like yesterday?" They simply do not know, for yesterday caught them by surprise.

Then, as if on cue, the conversation begins to fade—replaced with preparations for a second day in Jerusalem.

Jesus stops briefly to look around as He passes the last dwelling at the edge of the village—Bethany, the place that has become so special to Him and the place where He will lodge again tonight. The pause is brief, and the look on His face is almost melancholy. However, He does not permit the pause for but a brief moment. Jesus needs to be in Jerusalem.

As He turns His attention back to the pathway, the disciples are visiting amongst themselves. It is hard to tell if their placid gait is simply tiredness from yesterday or if it is the peace they feel so often when with Jesus. For whatever reason, the walk is relaxed and pleasant—for all but Jesus. Is this a calm before the certain storm that is continuing to build?

The morning sun, lifting from the east, illuminates the walls of Jerusalem in a spectacular, glistening display as the procession comes over the ridge of the Mount of Olives. However, it is the Temple, with its facades covered with golden plates, that steals the light of a new day most. Jesus looks that way—toward the city. He has always taken such pleasure from His creation. The awaking of nature in the morning, the coolness of the evening, the brightness of the midday heat, the solitude of nighttime—all bring Him such joy, and it is often easy to see it on His face.

However, this morning, is Jesus enjoying His creation as He looks over the city, or is the magnitude of the days ahead squeezing out everything else? After all, Jesus's days as a man are winding down. His purpose as the Savior will soon be fulfilled. His time to prepare those around Him for life without their Master is rapidly slipping through the hourglass. Yes, Jesus is feeling the crunch of time, and He is ready to embrace today! He glances back at those with Him as if to say, "Let's pick up the pace a little." A gentle glance over the shoulder saves the need for words.

The trip to the north ridge of the Mount of Olives is familiar and yet so different than it was yesterday. Today, the crowds are gone, save a few curious ones. And now they can enjoy this stretch of the road—the segment that has become their favorite. The final bend that has been shielding the city from view has finally been traversed, and each time, getting that fresh look at Jerusalem is as exhilarating as the first time they traveled this way.

Just like yesterday, as they draw near Mount Olivet, Bethphage quietly sits to the right. Its name in Hebrew means "House of Unripe Figs," and this certainly is the home of fig trees—lots of them. The trees are not only prevalent in the village, but they also dot the fields and line the road all around for quite a distance. But only one of them has drawn the attention of Jesus.

Jesus points off in the distance to a fig tree covered with leaves, and He heads that way. One of the disciples who is following Jesus draws near and says to no one in particular, "Jesus is hungry." Those closest by the Master must have heard Him say so as well—for they, in unison, nod their head in agreement. Jesus is hungry.

As Jesus approaches the fig tree, He carefully examines it and finds no fruit. Even though small figs appear on a fig tree before its leaves appear, this particular tree only has leaves. It is not the season for figs to be ripe, but there should be young figs visible amongst its leaves. The figs always appear before the leaves. This tree has none.

Almost as if on cue, many of the disciples begin to scurry to other trees, examining them for fruit—fruit that the Master may eat. They each call out as they find a tree bearing fruit, "I found one. Here, over here, there is fruit here." With the jubilation of a child at an egg hunt, the disciples point out each source of fruit they have located. But Jesus does not respond to their call—save an occasional glance their way.

Jesus simply speaks to the tree in an audible voice, *Let no one eat fruit from you ever again* (Mark 11:14a). That is all He says. There is no anger in His voice. There are no further comments. There are no instructions to the disciples to find Him something to eat. His only words are judgment on the tree. And Jesus remains hungry.

Jesus then turns away and continues on the path to Jerusalem. The disciples pause in bewilderment for a moment, looking at each other for a possible explanation. When none is offered, they respond to each other with a shrug and then hurry to catch up with Jesus—who is moving quickly and is almost out of sight.

Let us pause for a moment. We have now come upon an event in history that for many has warranted a name. They call it "Fig Monday." The brief yet unique encounter between Jesus and a fig tree has challenged and divided many scholars throughout the ages concerning the purpose and meaning of this encounter.

There are two parts to the story—this one today and the conclusion tomorrow. We are combining the two parts for continuity, clarity, and completeness. Part I happens today. Part II happens tomorrow.

The event is recorded in both Matthew and Mark. For our purposes, we will use the more extensive recording from Mark's gospel. Here is what Mark tells us:

> *Now the next day, when they had come out from Bethany, He was hungry. And seeing from afar a fig tree having leaves, He went to see if perhaps He would find something on it. When He came to it, He found nothing but*

> *leaves, for it was not the season for figs. In response Jesus said to it,* **"Let no one eat fruit from you ever again."** *And His disciples heard it."*
>
> – Mark 11:12-14

To summarize what Mark tells us:

- They are traveling from Bethany.
- Jesus is hungry.
- He spots a fig tree.
- He finds only leaves—no sign of fruit.
- He curses or pronounces a judgment on the tree.
- The disciples hear exactly what Jesus said.

Tomorrow (about the same time): Part II

As they continue on the path to Jerusalem, the fig tree of yesterday is buried deep in their memory. Some are replaying yesterday's event in the Temple and the resulting uneasiness they are feeling. Others are trying to figure out what today will hold. And still others are simply enjoying the walk. Jesus walks along in silence, alone with His thoughts and the tension that continues to build by the day and even by the hour.

However, as they approach the area of figs, Jesus's encounter with the tree is snapped back into their conscious as a startled Peter stops suddenly, stunned by what he sees. The excitement on his face and in his voice is classic Peter: *Rabbi, look! The fig tree which you cursed has withered away* (Mark 11:21b).

Those who are close by look in amazement at the scene before their eyes. Those who had wandered to the other side of the road come running across to see what the sudden commotion is about. The gospel of Matthew puts it this way: *And when the disciples saw it, **they marveled**, saying, "How did the fig tree wither away so soon?"* (Matthew 21:20).

Look at the disciples. The expressions pressed onto their faces are as diverse as their personalities. Mouths are wide open as jaws drop, eyes blink in wonderment, hands are waving about in excitement—and thoughts are being short-circuited. Thomas wonders if this is the same place as yesterday and the same tree. He looks around several times—trying to get his bearings.

Matthew said, "They marveled." Yes, they are! Yes, they are marveling! And their hearts echo words spoken centuries before: *Marvelous are Your works, and that my soul knows very well* (Psalm 139:14b). Once again, the mighty works of the Master astounds them.

Again, let us bring in Mark's account of today, the second day of the story:

> *Now in the morning, as they passed by, they saw the fig tree dried up from the roots. And Peter, remembering, said to Him, "Rabbi, look! The fig tree which You cursed has withered away." So Jesus answered and said to them, "Have faith in God. For assuredly, I say to you, whoever says to this mountain, 'Be removed and be cast into the sea,' and does not doubt in his heart, but believes that those things he says will be done, he will have whatever he says. Therefore I say to you, whatever things you ask when you pray, believe that you receive them, and you will have them. And whenever you stand praying, if you have anything against anyone, forgive him, that your Father in heaven may also forgive you your trespasses. But if you do not forgive, neither will your Father in heaven forgive your trespasses."*

– Mark 11:20-26

To summarize what Mark tells us about Part II of the encounter:

- It's the next day.
- They see the tree dried from its roots.
- Peter exclaims it to Jesus.
- Jesus seizes the moment to teach them about faith and forgiveness.

While Jesus's encounter with the fig tree has much symbolism in it, such as the fig tree representing Israel and the expectations of producing fruit, is it not somewhat ironic that Jesus is using this moment to teach His disciples about faith and forgiveness?

Jesus's response to Peter and the others is: *Have **faith** in God...And whenever you stand **pray**ing, if you have anything against anyone, **forgive** him* (Mark 11:22b, 25a, 25b). Wow, faith in God and prayer and forgiving others! Jesus knows time is short and He is teaching—preparing—equipping. A withered fig tree? That is nothing. But having faith in God—well, that is everything!

Ironic? No not at all! For very soon the disciples' faith will be tested, challenged, and through the power of the Holy Spirit, increased.

(Return to today)

Coming up to the eastern gates of Jerusalem is always an exhilarating feeling. It provides a sense of arriving. Often times, the trip has been long for the travelers. At best, it is tiring and, at worse, dangerous and perilous—a favorite location for thieves. While at the floor of the Kidron Valley, looking eastward, the massive walls of Jerusalem dominate the view. The climb seems to always be longer and steeper than it actually is. It certainly seems that way to those making the climb right now.

Jesus clears the crest of the hill, looks up at the massive Golden Gates, and passes through the thick, gated walls of the city—leading into the Temple. He turns and pauses briefly to make sure all are still with Him and then places His full attention toward the Temple.

For His disciples, coming into Jerusalem just now is a source of uneasiness. The events of yesterday, the obvious disdain of the Pharisees—who have been their constant shadow—and the stir that follows Jesus everywhere—have unsettled them, to be sure. Somehow this trip to Jerusalem for Passover feels different. A few even wish this Feast were over so they could head back to Galilee to a much more familiar and safer place.

Palm Sunday to Resurrection Sunday

Little do they know there will be no more Galilean hillsides for them—listening to Jesus teach.

The sound that greets them, as they harness their attention and direct it to the activity surrounding them, is the noise of busyness and business. It is not a loud noise filled with the yells or screams of a joyous gathering. It is just noise—the sound of people—lots of people, all frantically or diligently doing what they had come here to do—some to buy, some to sell, some to find a bargain on an animal, some to steal, and some to cheat. But none are there just to hang out—not even the sinister ones lurking in the shadows, waiting for their opportunity. And it challenges one to sort out the source of each sound.

They are in the outer courts of the Temple—that vast area of space called the Court of the Gentiles. In this area of the temple—removed from the Court of Israel and the Holy Place (and certainly the Holy of Holies)—necessary business is transacted.

The disciples, while staying close to Jesus, look around at the volume of activity in front of them—seemingly endless acres of booths, tables, and restless animals. It feels like everyone is moving together—in opposite directions—appearing to certainly crash together in a massive pile—but never doing so. Even those who have stopped to barter or buy seem to be moving, though they are not.

The smells, forcing their way into the consciousness of everyone, are captivating. Yesterday there was a breeze that imported the smells from the surrounding areas. The wet smell of animals being purified, the smell of freshly spilt blood, and the exposed flesh of the animals being sacrificed and burnt for atonement came crashing in from other parts in the Temple. Even the soft smell of unleavened bread and the aroma of a fresh cooked meal crept over the Temple walls to temper the stronger odors.

But today, the air is still and stagnant, and the aroma of goats, sheep, cattle, and doves (and their dung) mingle with the odor of the weary, worn traveler as he passes by. It borders on being a stench. However, no one seems to pay attention or care.

All of this is a repeat of yesterday, when the disciples dutifully tagged along as Jesus methodically and tediously examined each and every aspect of the Temple—except where even He was not permitted. The time was seemingly long, if not actually several hours, and the disciples had plenty of time to be entertained by the activities in the Temple and maybe were even a little bored.

But today is different because Jesus is different. Yesterday, the Master slowly and deliberately moved about making mental notes. However, today, He seems to be more on a mission—and it makes the disciples uneasy.

Jesus has a presence about Him that does not go unnoticed, and today, people are drawn from their tasks, pausing to watch this Nazarene. Some, just yesterday, had palm branches in their hands. Others are merchants frustrated with the pause of trading—fidgeting like a businessman late for a meeting. Even those who are strangers pause to watch what Jesus will do or say. And the sinister begin to move at this opportunity. However, the most interested of all are the Pharisees, shadowing Jesus to see what He would do next. It didn't take long.

Again, we best tell the story through the scriptures:

- *Then Jesus went into the temple of God and drove out all those who bought and sold in the temple, and overturned the tables of the money changers and the seats of those who sold doves. **And He said to them**, "It is written, 'My house shall be called a house of prayer,' but you have made it a 'den of thieves'"* (Matthew 21:12-13).
- *So they came to Jerusalem. Then Jesus went into the temple and began to drive out those who bought and sold in the temple, and overturned the tables of the money changers and the seats of those who sold doves. And He would not allow anyone to carry wares through the temple. Then He taught, **saying to them**, "Is it not written, 'My house shall be called a house of prayer for all nations'? But you have made it a 'den of thieves.'" And the scribes and chief priests heard it and sought how they might destroy Him; for they feared Him, because all the people were astonished at His teaching. When evening had come, He went out of the city* (Mark 11:15-19).
- *Then He went into the temple and began to drive out those who bought and sold in it, **saying to them**, "It is written, 'My house is a house of prayer,' but you have made it a 'den of thieves'"* (Luke 19:45-46).

A normal day in the Temple at Passover has just been ripped from its foundation. Jesus is angry, and it cannot be sugar coated. The mental notes of yesterday have become a gigantic call to action—and Jesus is up to the task.

There is no need for violent action. There are no fists flying between Jesus and those He is driving out of the Temple. There is no resistance to His commands and actions. This is the Commanding Jesus. This is the One who spoke to the winds and the waves, and they were silent. This is the One who commanded Peter to walk on the open water, and he did. This is the One who stopped a lifetime flow of blood. This is the One who commanded demons to leave a possessed man, and they asked for permission to dwell elsewhere. This is God righting a wrong.

The abuse of His Father's house is breaking Jesus's heart, and as He commands it to cease, people are fleeing through the Temple gates; Jesus is turning over the vacated tables and coin boxes and unlatching the bird cages—then opening them. The House of God needs cleansing, and it is a mission rapidly being accomplished.

The disciples at first stand stunned, then feebly hover around Jesus as though they are reluctant bodyguards. The sinister grasp at fleeing doves and spring upon fallen coins, and anger grows deeper and deeper in the hearts of the scribes and chief priests. And they further plot to kill Jesus.

The people have not left the outer courts of the Temple, at least not totally. They simply are scattering from an angry Jesus. Jesus has separated them from their workplace. He has driven them from the spot where they have been desecrating His Father's house. And He is not completely finished.

As Jesus continues, the people are staying a safe distance away, but not hiding in terror. This is not a lunatic on the loose. This is not a wild man possessed. This is not even one who has lost his temper. Rather, this is the Correcting Parent.

They stand securely behind Temple columns or each other—then slowly, creep ever closer to watch. They maneuver to get a better viewpoint—all apprehensive, yet somehow all being drawn to this Jesus of Nazareth.

The disciples, now somewhat recovered from their initial shock, study Jesus's face for clues of understanding. They have seen Him upset before. They had seen Jesus become angry at the Pharisees when they chastised Him for healing a man's withered hand on the Sabbath in Capernaum, and they remember in the region of Caesarea Philippi when He had rebuked Peter with the words *Get behind Me, Satan!* (Luke 4:8) But this is different. This whole week has been different, and the disciples are very unsettled as they struggle to sort out the scene that is unfolding in front of them.

The crowd also is trying to measure the mood of Jesus. What they are witnessing is not a madman gone wild. It is not the acts of one struggling with deep anger issues. It is not hatred manifesting itself in an uncontrolled rage.

No! This is the look of a saddened Father who knows His child must be corrected. This is the pain of disappointment that can no longer be suppressed. This is shortening the leash of a wayward child. This is love mixed with the demand for justice. Jesus's grief at the treatment of His Father's house is demanding action. And action it is receiving.

The Court of the Gentiles is a very large area, and as Jesus moves from one area to another, merchants and moneychangers cautiously, but hurriedly, scurry to retrieve their scattered wares. As Jesus moves about, the whole courtyard appears like an ocean wave working its way down the beach—first a crashing wave, then the rippling and backwashing effect that swirls in the wake of the wave that just passed through. It is the beach striving to return to normal. It is wet sand resettling and ocean foam bubbling next to a shocked seashell. All around, the beach hopes this is the last intruding wave—but knows it is not.

Jesus stops to speak. Look closely at the following verses:

- "He said to them" (Matthew 21:13).
- "Saying to them" (Mark 11:17).
- "Saying to them" (Luke 19:46).

These phrases as used by Matthew, Mark, and Luke in the text above have the same meaning. In the Greek, the word is "lego" (leg-o) and it means to lay forth, to systematically relate in words, to put forth, to tell, to utter.

Jesus is explaining His actions, and He is not yelling in a rage. In fact, Mark says Jesus is teaching. Nonetheless, His words are uncompromising and far from soft and gentle. The grief is still there, but the anger is subsiding and Jesus is teaching: *Then He taught, saying to them, "Is it not written, 'My house shall be called a house of prayer for all nations'? But you have made it a 'den of thieves.'"* (Mark 11:17).

Is it not written? Yes, it is written! It is written by the prophets. Isaiah 56:7 says, *Even them I will bring to My holy mountain, and make them joyful **in My house of prayer.*** And Jeremiah 7:11 asks, *Has this house, which is called by My name, become **a den of thieves** in your eyes?*

As Jesus speaks, His words are not the words of a defendant, for Jesus has no need to defend His actions. Rather, the Teacher so wants His listeners to "get it." He wants them to understand how holy is the ground on which they are standing. He wants them to have the affection for this Temple that it deserves. It is the Lord's house! But their dishonest trading is desecrating the house of the Lord, and it saddens Jesus.

All the while Jesus was cleansing the Temple, not one temple guard attempted to stop Him. No Roman soldiers came around to investigate the cause of all of the commotion. Not one scribe, Pharisee, or temple worker raised a hand against Jesus. But why? Why did no one at least try to stop Him? It is because God was in the house—"My house of prayer!"

As He continues to teach in the outer courts of the Temple, a blind man is groping his way toward the voice. Some of the crowd is moving aside to let him by. But now, a man is taking his arm and leading him to Jesus. The blind man is calling out Jesus's name and begging Him to give him sight. He had heard that Jesus could give him sight—could He? And would He? The call of the man continues until he is face to blind face with Jesus. Though he cannot see Him, he knows he is in the presence of the Healer.

Of course, Jesus can heal him. And, of course, Jesus does just that. He draws the man to Himself and touches him. Immediately, the complex design of sight is restored. No high-tech surgeries are required— no patches over eyes for healing—just the touch of the Healing Jesus.

The man, for just a moment, stands in wonderment as images, now unblocked, enter his eyes and begin to register in his brain. He blinks, and for the first time, he has faces to put with familiar voices. He looks into the eyes of Jesus. The face of Jesus is the first image his eyes have ever beheld, and the man's eyes are riveted. The moment is brief, yet its impact is eternal as the eyes of gratitude meet the eyes of the Master and for this man—formerly blind—love and compassion have just been redefined.

He then turns to those around him, those who brought him here, and the man softly whispers, "They don't look anything like I envisioned. They are all so beautiful!" He blinks often, his whole system being recalibrated to this new world before him—a world not just of sounds and smells, but rather a wonderful new world—in glorious, living color.

The crowd is now silent, save the distant sounds of the return of bartering. As more and more images captivate the man, the initial shock of seeing eases and the man is no longer simply standing there. He is running and jumping, waving his arms, yelling and laughing and hugging his friends as he looks into their eyes for the very first time.

His commotion has attracted the attention of that part of the courtyard, and others are gathering to watch. Jesus smiles as suddenly all of those who had come to the Temple today hoping for a miracle are being brought His way. He sees them, He has compassion for them, and He gives sight to the blind and He heals the lame.

Cleansing, correcting, teaching, healing—it is just what Jesus does.

Indignant. That is what Matthew calls them. However, it may be too docile a word to describe the emotions boiling within the chief priests and scribes. For way too long now, they have been watching the "wonderful things" Jesus has been doing throughout the Temple. And they are steaming!

The children are running and playing in the courtyard. On their lips is the joyous chant of "Hosanna to the Son of David!" "Hosanna to the Son of David!" Over and over, the children call out the words—first one of them, then several, then all in unison as they weave around the towering columns of the Court of the Gentiles. It is not really a chant. It is more a combination of sheer joy, unbridled laughter, singing, and youthful excitement. The children are bounding around, full of energy that is being drawn from an endless reservoir. Those who have just been healed are clapping and cheering them on. Their family and friends are just as enthusiastic, and others join in—encouraging the praise of Jesus—indeed, "Hosanna to the Son of David." And the indignation grows.

The squirrel is barking at the grizzly again, and Matthew tells us what follows:

> *But when the chief priests and scribes saw the wonderful things that He did, and the children crying out in the temple and saying, "Hosanna to the Son of David!" they were indignant and said to Him, "Do You hear what these are saying?" And Jesus said to them, "Yes, have you never read, 'Out of the mouth of babes and nursing infants You have perfected praise'?"*

– Matthew 21:15-16

The chief priests and scribes are painted in a corner. Jesus has become a major problem. He is gaining many followers. He is doing many wonders. And on their challenges concerning the Law of Moses, the scribes have lost them all. They would love to be rid of Him, but they fear the people. Much discussion has yielded no feasible plan of extermination—so they continue to fume and be indignant. Again, the squirrel's bark waxes cold.

Jesus and the disciples head back to Bethany, and Day Two closes under a clear, sparkling, and starry night.

LIFE APPLICATION

You did not choose Me, but I chose you and appointed you that you should go and bear fruit, and that your fruit should remain, that whatever you ask the Father in My name He may give you (John 15:16).

Create in me a clean heart, O God, and renew a steadfast spirit within me (Psalm 51:10).

Jesus looked for fruit from the fig tree. Finding none, He passed judgment on it, and the tree never bore fruit again. We, as Christians, are expected to bear fruit. The Apostle Paul in Galatians gives us an idea of what our fruit should look like: *But the fruit of the Spirit is love, joy, peace, longsuffering, kindness, goodness, faithfulness, gentleness, self-control. Against such there is no law* (Galatians 5:22-23). James 3:8 talks about the fruit of righteousness, and Hebrews 13:15 about the fruit of our lips. Romans 7:14 tells us we should bear our fruit to God, and John 15:8 says our good fruit glorifies God.

Question: If you are a Christian, are you bearing good fruit? Take a measure of yourself today and ask God to produce more fruit in you in the areas you may be weakest. He will help you to do so.

Jesus cleansed the Temple because people were desecrating it and it needed cleansing. Jesus had come in and examined the Temple first—then He cleansed it. The Bible tells us that we too need cleansing. Here are a few examples:

- Unrighteousness (1 John 1:9).
- Hands (James 4:8).
- Conscience (Hebrews 9:14).
- Secret faults (Psalm 19:12).
- Evil (Proverbs 20:30).
- Iniquity (Ezekiel 36:33).

Question: Are you willing to let God get the dirt and the cobwebs from your heart? Can you, like David, ask the Lord to create a clean heart in you today? He desires to do so. Let Him clean your heart and repair your secret faults right now.

Chapter Five

> "The teaching of Jesus has had a power and effect with which the influence of no other teacher can even for a moment compare."
>
> James Stuart (Scottish Theologian)

When Jesus had finished these words, the crowds were amazed at His teaching (Matthew 7:28).

Passion Week – Day Three
Teaching Tuesday

Tuesday of Holy Week is the only day that has not been given a name down through history. Yet more of this day has found its way into scripture than any other day of Passion Week—save Friday. The day starts early in Bethany and ends late in the day on the Mount of Olives. And much of the day is filled with Jesus teaching—hence, we shall call today Teaching Tuesday.

Today will find Jesus being challenged four times by the religious leaders of Jerusalem. It will be their purpose to trap Jesus into saying something that may be held against Him. Each group of leaders takes their turn in a well-planned effort to paint Jesus into a theological corner.

First, there are the Chief Priests, Scribes, and Elders, then the Pharisees and Herodians. Next, the Sadducees are sent to challenge Jesus. And finally, a single scribe comes forth to question Him about the Greatest Commandment.

Today will also be filled with Jesus teaching in parables, exposing the hypocrisy of the religious leaders, and doing His best to prepare the disciples and people for what lies ahead in the coming days. The day will end with Jesus's lengthy end-times discourse, which has become known as the Olivet Discourse. While the day will be filled with tension and confrontation, mostly it is about Jesus teaching.

Jesus was a teacher, and He taught often. Later this morning at the fig tree, He will teach His disciples about faith. The disciples will be marveling at the withered tree. They will stare at the tree, examine the tree—even look around to make sure it is the same tree Jesus cursed yesterday. But the miracle of a fig tree withering so quickly is not the story Jesus wants the disciples to grasp. Rather, He has a truth He wants them to comprehend, for He knows they will need to draw upon it in the coming days. So, He teaches them. We looked at this story in the previous chapter—combining the events of yesterday with the second part of the story as it occurs today. The message of Jesus's teaching? *Have faith in God* (Mark 11:22b).

Jesus's renown as a teacher has spurred so much critical analysis that it has even led to the dissecting of His style by the theological and educational communities. Scholars have examined how His charisma and persona enhanced His effectiveness as a teacher. In addition, they have studied His:

- Psychological strategies
- Philosophy
- Use of parables
- Use of allegories
- Use of figurative utterances
- Use of rhetoric in moral teaching
- Style of moral teaching
- Authoritative skills

Scholars have even discussed the influence of Socrates on His teaching style and the fact that His teaching was entirely oral—there are no literary works from Jesus. But one thing is certain—Jesus taught:

- *He opened His mouth **and began to teach them**, saying:* (Matthew 5:2).
- *For He was **teaching them as one having authority**, and not as their scribes* (Matthew 7:29).
- *So **He began to teach them many things*** (Mark 6:34b).
- *And He **taught in their synagogues**, being glorified by all* (Luke 4:15).
- *This man came to Jesus by night and said to Him, "Rabbi, we know that You are a **teacher come from God**; for no one can do these signs that You do unless God is with him"* (John 3:2).
- *Then **He taught them many things by parables*** (Mark 4:2a).
- *Jesus answered them and said, **"doctrine is not Mine, but His who sent Me"*** (John 7:16).

Jesus was acknowledged as a teacher. His acclaim as a teacher has not been questioned. His deity has been questioned. His position as the Messiah has been questioned. Even His existence has been questioned. But not His title of Teacher:

- **Jesus Called Himself Teacher** – *You call Me Teacher and Lord, and you say well, **for so I am**. If I then, your Lord and **Teacher**, have washed your feet, you also ought to wash one another's feet* (John 13:13-14).
- **Jesus Instructed Peter and John to call Him Teacher** – *Then you shall **say** to the master of the house, "**The Teacher** says to you, 'Where is the guest room where I may eat the Passover with My disciples?'"* (Luke 22:11).
- **Mary Called Him Teacher** – *Jesus said to her, "Mary!" She turned and said to Him, "Rabboni!" (which is to say, **Teacher**)* (John 20:16).
- **Martha Called Him Teacher** – *And when she had said these things, she went her way and secretly called Mary her*

sister, saying, "The **Teacher** has come and is calling for you" (John 11:28).

- **Nicodemus Called Him Teacher** – *This man came to Jesus by night and said to Him, "Rabbi, we know that **You are a teacher come from God; for no one can do these signs that You do unless God is with him"* (John 3:2).
- **The Rich Young Ruler Called Him Teacher** – *Now a certain ruler asked Him, saying, "**Good Teacher,** what shall I do to inherit eternal life?"* (Luke 18:18).
- **The Multitude Called Him Teacher** – *Then one from the crowd said to Him, "**Teacher,** tell my brother to divide the inheritance with me"* (Luke 12:13).
- **The Disciples of John Called Him Teacher** – *Then Jesus turned, and seeing them following, said to them, "What do you seek?" They said to Him,* ***"Rabbi" (which is to say, when translated, Teacher),*** *"where are You staying?"* (John 1:38).
- **The Sadducees Called Him Teacher** – *Saying: "**Teacher,** Moses wrote to us that if a man's brother dies, having a wife, and he dies without children, his brother should take his wife and raise up offspring for his brother"* (Luke 20:28).
- **The Chief Priest and Scribes Called Him Teacher** – *Then they asked Him, saying, "**Teacher,** we know that **You** say and **teach rightly,** and You do not show personal favoritism, **but teach the way of God in truth:"*** (Luke 20:21).

Seventy-two times in the New Testament, Jesus was called Teacher, Rabbi, or Rabboni. He was known as **The Teacher.** Jesus even explained to the multitudes that there is but One who is their Teacher: *But you, do not be called "Rabbi"; for* ***One is your Teacher, the Christ,*** *and you are all brethren* (Matthew 23:8).

Jesus is indeed The Teacher, and today will be the last day He will ever teach in public.

Jesus concludes His words to the disciples, pauses to measure their comprehension, and then turns toward the road—His face set toward Jerusalem. Thomas takes one last look back, over his shoulder, at the withered tree, wondering how it could have died so quickly—seeking a logical explanation—but failing to find one. Similar thoughts and actions still linger with the others as well, but only for a moment. Peter is still marveling, talking, and waving his arms in typical Peter fashion, and John is trying to stay close to Jesus.

The dust of the path is springing to life in clouds around them as Jesus sets a brisk pace toward the city. Today's start seems a little earlier than yesterday, and the rising sun exposes an eerie haze of dust that is encapsulating them.

The curious are spellbound by the sight and barely move as Jesus and His disciples walk away, slowly disappearing in the fog—a dust fog. As the curious simply stand by watching, the disciples are losing ground to the quick-paced Jesus and are feeling rushed as they try to keep up. Things just feel weird.

Jesus's words about faith in God and removing a mountain and forgiving others are still ringing in the disciples' ears. Similar words they had heard before from Jesus. While in Galilee, the disciples had been asked by a man to heal his epileptic son. The disciples tried but could not do so. *Then the disciples came to Jesus privately and said, "Why could we not cast it out?" So Jesus said to them, "Because of your unbelief; for assuredly, I say to you, if you have faith as a mustard seed, you will* **say to this mountain, 'Move** *from here to there,' and it will move; and nothing will be impossible for you"* (Matthew 17:19-20).

They know Jesus is pointing out their unbelief—their lack of faith—even their selfishness and lack of forgiveness. But this time, it is different. There is urgency in Jesus's voice. It is as if Jesus is telling them, "Finals are coming soon, and this will be on the test." Jesus is different, the week is different, and the disciples are beginning to feel these are uncertain days. Their anxiety is building toward fear. The question in their minds: *What is coming next?*

Long before any thoughts are sorted out and settled, the disciples see Jesus passing through the shadows of the thick walls of the city. They hurry. They must not let Him disappear into the crowded streets alone. Things are too tenuous, and they must keep Him in sight and remain close at all times.

Familiar smells and sounds crash into their senses, and the energy that permeates Jerusalem at Passover is instantly snapping the disciples' minds to attention. No longer are they strolling along a dusty pathway or slowly digesting the words of the Master. Oh no, they are in the city now and rapidly absorbing everything their eyes and ears are capturing. They are alert—they are cautious—they are nervous.

People know when Jesus is close by. They just do. It has always been that way. Maybe today it is His entourage of disciples or the murmurs in the crowd. Maybe there has been so much talk about Jesus all around the streets of Jerusalem that some have just come to get a glimpse of this man from Nazareth. But since Jesus's arrival a couple of days ago, there is much more buzz surrounding Him than normal. The presence of Jesus captivates people. It always has.

Jesus enters the temple and immediately begins to teach: *He taught the people in the temple and preached the gospel* . . . (Luke 20:1a). Oh, how Jesus loves to teach. Gone is the anger of yesterday. Gone is the triumphal entry. Gone is the fig tree. Gone even is much of the urgency within Jesus as His destiny with the cross draws closer. Today is a day for teaching, and Jesus embraces the moment.

As He walks through the temple, people are gathering and listening. His words are riveting, and the crowds grow—if not swell—quickly as Jesus continues to move throughout the Court of the Gentiles. Rapidly, people are becoming aware of the presence of Jesus, and their words—sometimes whispers but often shouts—are spreading throughout the courtyard: "The Teacher is here!"

The disciples begin to relax. They too are gripped by the words of Jesus—words that are filled with so much truth and compassion and regard for His listeners that people are astonished. Flashbacks of Jesus teaching on a Galilean hillside and men climbing in trees to listen and the offer of salvation beside a Samaritan well serve as an instant oasis of calm for the disciples as Jesus savors another precious moment to teach. Normalcy has returned. Or has it?

Just as quickly, the scene before them changes and the disciples' prior uneasiness has returned. Everyone is pausing—waiting to see what is about to unfold. The Roman soldiers are mused and curious as Jesus continues moving through the temple—continuing to teach—but not turning away as a large contingency of chief priests, scribes, and elders head directly His way. They have been waiting for Him. The wait is over.

Yesterday was a bad day for the Jewish clergy. Jesus's cleansing of the temple was a major embarrassment, and they are still reeling—even this morning. This was not simply another minor disruption by the problematic Nazarene—not this time.

This was instead a tsunami ripping through the temple, scattering everything and everyone, and nothing has settled back into its original, well-planned place. The financial loss of the day was great, and it has become a significant source of the hate that is building within them. Passover—a very lucrative time for the moneychangers and those who sell doves and their wares—this year is not yet seeing record profits, even though the crowds in the city are at or near record levels. Passover is **THE** time of the year—the time for large volumes and high profit margins and even thievery and dishonest gain. But Jesus has made this a terrible year for all the profiteers.

However, more troublesome to the Jewish leaders are the people. They are losing them. They are losing the strong hand of control. They are losing the unchallenged respect of their position. With every word or appearance of this man from Galilee, the people are cheering and listening and even worshipping Him. Oft time, the Pharisees are receiving little more than a polite nod or even a weak smile of acknowledgement. Their pride is being bruised, and disdain for Jesus has found a permanent home in the hearts of Jerusalem's religious leaders.

Yesterday's cheers from the crowd and the children singing praises of Hosanna to Jesus and the response of the crowds in the temple to His teaching are troublesome. Yesterday signaled a call to action for the chief priests: *And the scribes and chief priests heard it and **sought how they might destroy Him;** for they feared Him, because all the people were astonished at His teaching* (Mark 11:18).

Yesterday indeed was a bad day! Neither a sleepless night nor heated discussions throughout the night in search of a solution nor sinister plotting have done anything to sooth their anger and indignation.

Palm Sunday to Resurrection Sunday

The calmer and more honorable of the Pharisees have lost their argument to move cautiously and carefully. Instead, the centrifuge of anger boiling within most of the other leaders has won out—easily. Drastic action is required. The people's allegiance must return. The Nazarene must be stopped. Their power must be restored—and profits must return!

Jesus has stricken a blow to sin and hypocrisy. It has hit home with the scribes, and they are boiling with a hatred that will not diminish in the coming days. The final straw has broken the camel's back!

I wonder what Judas is thinking right now.

A full night of planning and scheming has yielded but one strategy, and in unison, the priests and scribes and elders are marching indignantly to Jesus to unpack their question. "What right do you have to do that?" or "Who do you think you are?" or "Who said you could . . . ?" is how twenty-first century America will ask the question much later. But today, it is: "By what authority?" *Now it happened on one of those days, as He taught the people in the temple and preached the gospel, that the chief priests and the scribes, together with the elders,* **confronted Him and spoke to Him, saying, "Tell us, <u>by what authority</u> are You doing these things? Or who is he who gave You this authority?"** (Luke 20:1-2).

The religious contingency has reached Jesus, just moments behind the question that they have been hurling His way repeatedly as they approach Him. They are cloaking themselves with all the "priestly" manners and control they can muster—working hard to look, behave, and maintain an appearance of strength and spiritual authority. They are failing terribly.

The disciples shift uneasily around the Master, not knowing for sure what to do. They have never had to physically defend Jesus before:

- **Not on the precipice** overlooking Nazareth when His neighbors wanted to cast Jesus over the edge. There, they just walked away as the people lifted not a finger against Him.
- **Not in the presence of the demon-possessed man**—so out of control and menacing. Granted, that was a little unsettling. But

Jesus spoke, and the demons asked for permission to enter swine instead. The wild man became normal.
- **Not from the swarming crowds.** Oh, there were times when they were surrounded on all sides. That was a little uncomfortable. There was even the time when Jesus taught from a boat to keep the people at a distance. But no real trouble there.
- **Not even previously from the ever-present and ever-stalking Pharisees and scribes.** Yes, they always challenged and questioned Jesus. Yes, they were obviously troubled by His words and miracles. Yes, they were afraid of the people who revered Jesus. But physical confrontation was never really an issue.

However, is this time different? After all, this whole trip to Jerusalem has been filled with surprises and uncertainty. They don't know for sure, so they wait and watch anxiously—very anxiously.

The contrast is unavoidable. On one side of the battle line is the contingency of religious leaders—the elite. Sweaty brows, red faces, and bulging veins expose the dark spiritual cloud of hate, anger, and disdain within them. Here, a combative and confrontational spirit boils at their very core. Here, self-promotion has taken up the sword of aggression. Hovering over them is a cloud—a dark cloud indeed.

Standing in front of the priests, scribes, and elders is Jesus. His pained face reveals the sadness within as He looks upon this group of leaders—the men chosen to shepherd His Father's people. These are the ones given the authority of instituting the Law of Moses. These men have been charged with leading the people into the obedience and worship of the Lord. But this noble profession has become contaminated with hypocrisy and greed for power and money. And Jesus is grieving, for He knows today will be His last chance to help them see their sin.

So, He slows their aggression by answering them with a question they dare not answer. Mark tells us the story:

> *But Jesus answered and said to them, "I also will ask you one question; then answer Me, and I will tell you by what authority I do these things: The baptism of John— was it from heaven or from men? Answer Me." And they reasoned among themselves, saying, "If we say, 'From*

> *heaven,' He will say, 'Why then did you not believe him?' But if we say, 'From men'" — they feared the people, for all counted John to have been a prophet indeed. So they answered and said to Jesus, "We do not know." And Jesus answered and said to them, "Neither will I tell you by what authority I do these things."*
>
> – Mark 11:29-33

The quickness with which Jesus disarms the Jewish leaders has brought a stir to the disciples and the crowd watching. Even some of the vendors pause to watch the leaders squirm. The Roman soldiers are amused.

However, Jesus is here to teach. Discarded is the ill-intended question concerning His authority, and Jesus seizes the opportunity to help the leaders recognize and acknowledge their sin. The priests stand stunned and still frustrated. The disciples remain cautious. The gathering crowds are trying to understand what is happening, and the Roman soldiers remain amused.

This encounter is the first of four challenges the leaders have contrived in an effort to trap Jesus. But this is a day of teaching for Jesus, and He immediately uses three parables to expose their hypocrisy and help the priests, scribes, and elders see their sinful ways:

- The Parable of the Two Sons
- The Parable of the Wicked Vinedresser
- The Parable of the Wedding Feast

Note: It is not our purpose to unpack the meaning of any of the parables or teachings of Jesus today. Many have already accomplished that task. Rather, our goal, as defined in our introduction, is to bring us to the events as though we are there—experiencing the emotions, tensions, and excitement of each day.

As Jesus speaks, the crowds that have gathered are listening intently—attempting to glean what they can from the Master. The disciples, likewise, are seeking the meaning of each story. Even some of the Roman soldiers appear to be listening intently.

But the religious leaders have already chosen not to hear, nor will they perceive the message—thus fulfilling the words of Jesus in Mark 4:12, words spoken by Isaiah centuries earlier: *So that "Seeing they may see and not perceive, And hearing they may hear and not understand; Lest they should turn, And their sins be forgiven them."*

The mood of the religious leaders has far surpassed frustration and annoyance. It is no longer a game of political maneuvering. It is no longer one-upmanship for power and influence over the people. The hate within them is building as Jesus's appointed time on the cross draws nearer. But today is not that day, even though we are told, *And they sought to lay hands on Him, but feared the multitude, for they knew He had spoken the parable against them. So they left Him and went away* (Mark 12:12).

As Jesus continues to teach, His adversaries have retreated around the corner and out of sight—regrouping for their next assault. It would be easy at this point to paint the religious leaders as weak and pathetic. The fact that they are overmatched against Jesus is not a reason for condemnation. Their pride and greed for power and authority have made them pawns in the greatest spiritual battle of all time. But Jesus does not see them as adversaries. For the price of their sins this day, Jesus will die not many days hence.

The next challenge comes from the Pharisees and the Herodians. Their tactics have changed, their demeanor has changed, and their verbiage has changed—but their purpose has not changed:

- *So they watched Him, **and sent spies who pretended to be righteous,** that they might seize on His words, in order to deliver Him to the power and the authority of the governor* (Luke 20:20).
- *And they sent to Him their disciples with the Herodians, saying, "Teacher, we know that You are true, and teach the way of God in truth; nor do You care about anyone, for You do not regard the person of men. **Tell us, therefore, what do You think?** Is it lawful to pay taxes to Caesar, or not?"* (Matthew 22:16-17).

The Pharisees are playing games of deception with Jesus, but Jesus is no more deceived by the Pharisees than He was by the chief priests. Look how clearly Jesus exposes their fraud:

- *But Jesus perceived their wickedness, and said, "Why do you test Me, you hypocrites?"* (Matthew 22:18).
- *But He, knowing their hypocrisy, said to them, "Why do you test Me?"* (Mark 12:15).
- *But He perceived their craftiness, and said to them, "Why do you test Me?"* (Luke 20:23).

With every test, there are efforts to cause Jesus to stumble. Questions with seeming unanswerable answers are answered. Questions about paying taxes to Caesar and the resurrection of the dead and the first and greatest commandment are asked by all of the religious leaders of Jerusalem—each taking their turn—the priests, scribes, and elders—then the Pharisees and Herodians—then the Sadducees and finally another scribe.

As each question and event unfolds, an evil storm is brewing. With each failure to trick Jesus, hate and envy and discontent build. Jerusalem is given the opportunity to grasp the significance of this Passover Feast. Fulfillment of awaited prophesy is unfolding before their eyes. But Jerusalem will not see. Their conflicted and wayward spiritual leaders will soon lead the people, who are captivated by Jesus, astray with the shout of "Crucify Him!"

As this day unfolds, there are more parables. There are warnings by Jesus as He pronounces, "Woe," to the scribes and the Pharisees. As this day unfolds, Jesus is teaching about the widow and her mite. Jesus questions the priests concerning David and why he called His descendent Lord. And now we see Jesus lamenting over Jerusalem.

During the day, the questions change, the people move about—some coming nearer, others drifting away—and Jesus pours Himself into His teaching. The disciples watch the tension dissipate as the day wears on. But the disdain within the religious leaders is not waning. Jesus has easily dismantled their efforts and plans to attack Him, trick Him, and deceive Him. And now, there appears to be weariness within them—exhaustion brought on by failure and disappointment.

As the day rapidly fades, people begin to drift away. The scribes and Pharisees and priests remain—but only in the background. They struggle to see a solution to this problem—but for a violent end.

As we recount this day of teaching, we should not be overly consumed with the religious leaders and their conflicts with Jesus. Weaved within the drama is an amazing day of teaching and preaching by Jesus. It will be His last. The gospel writers give us a balanced picture of this day of teaching:

- *When they had heard these words, **they marveled**, and left Him and went away* (Matthew 22:22).
- *And when the multitudes heard this, **they were astonished** at His teaching* (Matthew 22:33).
- *And **no one was able to answer Him** a word, nor from that day on did anyone dare question Him anymore* (Matthew 22:46).
- *And the common people **heard Him gladly*** (Mark 12:37b).
- *But they could not catch Him in His words in the presence of the people. And **they marveled at His answer** and kept silent* (Luke 20:26).
- *Then some of the scribes answered and said, **"Teacher, You have spoken well."** But after that they dared not question Him anymore* (Luke 20:39-40).

The day in Jerusalem is over. As Jesus and His disciples head back to Bethany, they stop on the Mount of Olives—overlooking the temple. This surely is a special time for Jesus. It is just He and His disciples. Matthew tells us Peter, James, John, and Andrew privately begin to ask the meaning of these teachings.

Jesus's answer has become known as the Olivet Discourse—a lengthy teaching on end-times: *Take heed that no one deceive you*; *And the gospel must first be preached to all nations*; *For false christs and false prophets will arise*; *Heaven and earth shall pass away, but My words by no means shall pass away* (Mark 13:5,10,22,31).

The day ends with a quiet return to Bethany.

LIFE APPLICATION

And when the Sabbath had come, <u>He began to teach</u> in the synagogue. And many hearing Him were astonished, saying, "Where did this Man get these things? And what wisdom is this which is given to Him, that such mighty works are performed by His hands!" **(Mark 6:2).**

But the Helper, the Holy Spirit, whom the Father will send in My name, <u>He will teach you</u> all things, and bring to your remembrance all things that I said to you **(John 14:26).**

Not every teacher is a good teacher. Nor does every teacher teach truth. Nor does everyone listen to the message being taught. Nor is every message an important life lesson. Some teaching is just information—not necessarily bad information—but information for the data bank.

Jesus taught life lessons. The Bible does not record Him teaching the size of the Temple or the length of the ark. But He did on this Teaching Tuesday speak passionately about faith, forgiveness, prayer, sacrifice, pride, reaping fruit, and harvesting and rendering to God the things that are God's.

<u>Question:</u> What are you learning as you listen to the Lord speak through His Word? Are you reading God's Word to learn or just to know? Are you gleaning valuable life messages from the Bible and the Holy Spirit?

Study to shew thyself approved unto God, a workman that needeth not to be ashamed, rightly dividing the word of truth **(2 Timothy 2:15, KJV).**

It is not enough to just read the Bible. Many things require study. Why? So that we may know truth and understand truth and share truth correctly.

<u>Question:</u> Do you study the things of God? His attributes? His love? His claims? Do you need to spend more time studying and meditating about God that you may "show yourself approved"? Today is the best day to start!

Chapter Six

> "We are not told; and we must not desire to be wise above what is written."
>
> Matthew Henry

And the chief priests and the scribes sought how they might take Him by trickery and put Him to death (Mark 14:1b).

Passion Week – Day Four
Silent Wednesday

The statement above by Matthew Henry is very wise counsel indeed. The events of Wednesday have largely been left from the pages of scripture—hence, the name Silent Wednesday. Therefore, we will tread lightly as we attempt to bring to life what this day may have been like for those who are key to the story.

Matthew's gospel tells us, *Now it came to pass, <u>when Jesus had finished all these saying,</u> that He said to His disciples, "You know that after two days is the Passover, and the Son of Man will be delivered up to be crucified"* (Matthew 26:1).

What were **all these sayings** Jesus had just finished? Most certainly, they were the teachings of Tuesday that concluded with Jesus sharing

His lengthy discourse on the Mount of Olives. Teaching Tuesday was at its end, and Jesus's teaching and preaching to the people had just come to a close. Never again would the multitudes gather to hear Jesus, although tomorrow He will impart many important things with His disciples as they share the Passover Feast. It will be a final download of important truths that will sustain the apostles in the days and weeks ahead.

But just now, Jesus immediately looks to the coming days: *And the Son of Man will be delivered up to be crucified*. All of these sayings are now complete, and Jesus knows what is ahead.

And now, it is the day that history calls Silent Wednesday or Spy Wednesday. Matthew records three events in verses 3 through 16 of chapter 26:

- A Plot to Kill Jesus
- The Anointing of Jesus at Bethany
- Judas Agrees to Betray Jesus

But did they happen on Wednesday or another day? You may want to study this subject and determine your own opinion. We will not do so as part of this study; however, remembering that the Hebrew day begins at sunset and that Jesus was returning to Bethany at the end of the day, it is reasonable to place these three events after sunset—hence, on Wednesday.

Even though there is significant disagreement among biblical scholars, the fact remains these events happened and are significant parts to this story—regardless of where one chooses to place them chronologically.

The first day of the Feast of Unleavened Bread is tomorrow, and today is a day of planning and preparing—logistically, physically, and spiritually. Historians and theologians will call it a day of rest. And well it may be. But we would err to call it a day of relaxation, lounging around, and socializing. There is far too much electricity in the air for that. The spiritual storm cloud is rapidly forming, and the battle for all eternity is looming just ahead.

Jesus is somewhere on a hillside, praying as the sun gently pierces the horizon and slowly squeezes out the darkness. The darkness has tried to conceal the evil planning of the chief priests and scribes and the tragic decision of Judas Iscariot, but truth and history have recorded their actions—exposing their deed for the ages.

It would be unwise to surmise what Jesus is praying about this morning. Surely, the prayers are different than they were on Palm Sunday—just a few days ago. However, stop just now and paint your own picture of what Jesus is praying. What do you think? Is He asking for strength for Himself? His disciples? The people who will be led astray by the religious leaders? Is He asking for forgiveness for His adversaries? Is He thinking of the Passover Feast of tomorrow? What or who do you think Jesus is talking to the Father about just now? It is hard to imagine what Jesus is experiencing on this day—at this moment—with all that is going on around Him. Wouldn't it be amazing if we had His prayers of this day as a model for when we are facing difficult times?

Today, there will be no crowds surrounding Jesus and His apostles. Today, there will be no chief priests or scribes. There will be no Pharisees or Sadducees or Herodians. There will be no trick questions or menacing Roman soldiers—no children to cradle in His arms or Temples to cleanse—or parables to teach—not today. Therefore, it is indeed a day of rest.

Jesus is weary. This journey to the cross began in Caesarea Philippi weeks ago, and the events of the last three days have drained His energy and emotions. We must never forget that Jesus was fully man (just like us) and fully God. The man side of Jesus is exhausted. So, Jesus starts the day being refreshed by the Father—through prayer. I wonder if He repeats the prayer He prayed on the mount when overlooking the Sea of Galilee—that prayer we call the Lord's Prayer:

> *Our Father, who art in heaven,*
> *Hallowed be thy Name,*
> *Thy kingdom come,*

Thy will be done,
On earth as it is in heaven.

Give us this day our daily bread.
And forgive us our trespasses,
As we forgive those
Who trespass against us.

And lead us not into temptation,
But deliver us from evil.

For Thine is the kingdom,
And the power, and the glory,
For ever. Amen.

– Matthew 6: 9-13.

Prayer rejuvenates the heart. Prayer refreshes the soul. Prayer heals the spirit. Prayer is the salve for a troubled spirit, and just now, Jesus needs this time of refreshing.

Sweet hour of prayer
Sweet hour of prayer
That calls me from a world of care
And bids me at my Father's throne
Make all my wants and wishes known
In seasons of distress and grief
My soul has often found relief
And oft escaped the tempter's snare
By Thy return, sweet hour of prayer

Poem by William Walford–1842
Music by William B. Bradbury–1861

Prayer was always present in Jesus's life. There are more than sixty-five mentions of Jesus praying in the Bible. Here are a few:

- **At His Baptism** – *It came to pass that Jesus also was baptized; and <u>while He prayed,</u> the heaven was opened* (Luke 3:21).
- **Before He Chose His Apostles** – *Now it came to pass in those days that <u>He went out to the mountain to pray,</u> and continued all night in prayer to God. And when it was day, He called His disciples to Himself; and from them He chose twelve whom He also named apostles* (Luke 6:12-13).
- **Before Feeding the Five Thousand** – *And Jesus took the loaves, and <u>when He had given thanks</u> He distributed them to the disciples, and the disciples to those sitting down; and likewise of the fish, as much as they wanted* (John 6:11).
- **In Gethsemane** – *Then Jesus came with them to a place called Gethsemane, and said to the disciples, "Sit here <u>while I go and pray over there</u>"* (Matthew 26:36).
- **For Peter** – *And the Lord said, "Simon, Simon! Indeed, Satan has asked for you, that he may sift you as wheat. <u>But I have prayed for you,</u> that your faith should not fail; and when you have returned to Me, strengthen your brethren"* (Luke 22:31-32).
- **When Alone** – *So He Himself <u>often withdrew into the wilderness and prayed</u>* (Luke 5:16).
- **At His transfiguration** – *<u>As He prayed,</u> the appearance of His face was altered, and His robe became white and glistening* (Luke 9:29).
- **In Deep Need** – *And being in agony, <u>He prayed more earnestly</u>* (Luke 22:44a).
- **On the Cross** – *<u>Then Jesus said,</u> "Father, forgive them, for they do not know what they do." And they divided His garments and cast lots* (Luke 23:34).

As Jesus retreats from His sanctuary of prayer and joins the others, there is a freshness to His spirit. Prayer does that—it just does!

On the right day, climbing the hill to the palace of Caiaphas can be a pleasant experience indeed. While the climb is steep, the rewards at the top are more than worth the effort. Sitting on the east side of Mount Zion, the palace affords one of the most spectacular views of the Mount of Olives and much of the city of Jerusalem. In view is the Kidron Valley, the vast walls of Jerusalem and the City of David to the right in the distance. The homes of the people and the steps to the South Wall of the City are easy to locate on the horizon. And watching the movement of people and carts and animals below fascinates the mind.

Oft times, visitors to Caiaphas's house have stood and overlooked the city while waiting for the High Priest to appear. It was a time to reflect, gather thoughts, or maybe even pray. It was a time of calm, serenity, and peace.

But today is not the right day!

Today, the visitors have far too much on their mind. Today, there is tension, fear, and anger. Today, aggression is colliding with uncertainty and even guilt. Today, there is a meeting to discuss Jesus.

This is not the first meeting to discuss this troublesome Jew from Nazareth, but this one has all of the signs of being the decisive one. This one includes the high priests, the scribes, and the elders—and it is being held here at the palace of Caiaphas, the High Priest.

As they begin to arrive, it is easy to see the cloud that hangs over them. Some walk alone, laboriously, with their head lowered—deep in troubling thought. Others climb the final steps up the hill with a resolute and defiant demeanor. Still others, two by two or in small groups, are walking slowly, talking together as though they are strategizing—and well they may be. This is not a day of calm, serenity, and peace. Scripture explains: *Then the chief priests, the scribes, and the elders of the people assembled at the palace of the high priest, who was called Caiaphas, and plotted to take Jesus by trickery and kill Him. But they said, "Not during the feast, lest there be an uproar among the people"* (Matthew 26:3-5).

They are here to consult, plan, scheme, conspire, and plot how they might capture and then kill Jesus. They have had enough of Jesus—but why? Why has Jesus been such a lightning rod to the Jewish leaders? Why do they hate Him? Why do they want to kill Him? Don Stewart, pastor and Christian apologist, gives us six reasons:

- The claims that He made – claimed to be God and Messiah
- The deeds that He did – healed the sick and forgave sin
- His threat to their religious system – exposed their hypocrisy
- His threat to their way of life – unstable situation with Romans
- The people with whom He socialized – common people/sinners
- The lack of respect He had for their religious traditions – He was grieved by the way they perverted the Sabbath with oppressive laws

Jesus has been interrupting their lives for a long time, and now, things are marching to a conclusion—and the Jewish leaders are plotting! Their issues with Jesus go back nearly three years, and their list of accusations grows.

Throughout Jesus's ministry, they were there—accusing, challenging, and condemning Him. We see it first near Capernaum, when Jesus heals and forgives the paralytic: *This man blasphemes!* (Matthew 9:3). When He called Matthew as a disciple: **"Why does your Teacher eat with** *tax collectors and sinners?* (Matthew 9:11). When He healed the mute, demon-possessed man: **"He cast out demons** *by ruler of demons* (Matthew 9:34). When Jesus taught of defilement within: **"Why do your disciples transgress** *the traditions of the elders?* (Matthew 15:2).

On and on, they challenged His authority, His deity, His understanding and obedience of the law. And with each event, their anger grew, their disdain grew, their hate grew, and their desire to destroy Jesus became an obsession.

As the meeting unfolds, there are few moderate opinions. There is minimal discussion, and predetermined plans have already been finalized. The room is filled with anger and animosity. Voices are raised as emotions burst out, and opinions are voiced as though they are attempting to convince themselves that their coming actions are righteous and justified.

Scripture does not record their plan—only their purpose. But their intent to delay this killing until after Passover will not be successful, for prophecy and God had other plans. Jesus will be the sacrificial lamb of this Passover. And the Lord is turning evil into good to fulfill prophesy and His holy and eternal purposes.

Palm Sunday to Resurrection Sunday

Across the Kidron Valley and back in Bethany, the scene is much different. Jesus is at the home of Simon, the leper:

> *And when Jesus was in Bethany at the house of Simon the leper, a woman came to Him having an alabaster flask of very costly fragrant oil, and she poured it on His head as He sat at the table. But when His disciples saw it, they were indignant, saying, "Why this waste? For this fragrant oil might have been sold for much and given to the poor." But when Jesus was aware of it, He said to them, "Why do you trouble the woman? For she has done a good work for Me. For in pouring this fragrant oil on My body, she did it for My burial. Assuredly, I say to you, wherever this gospel is preached in the whole world, what this woman has done will also be told as a memorial to her."*

– Matthew 26:6-13

Jesus is sitting at the table. It is an interesting picture to paint in our mind of Jesus. At this monumental moment in His life, knowing He is but a short time from an excruciating death, he is sitting and talking to those who are present at Simon's house today. We see the compassionate Jesus, the one who always cares for His own.

He knows their lives will soon be thrust into turmoil and confusion. He knows that these are the last minutes and hours that He will be with them. So, He sits at the table conversing with them.

Scripture records other times Jesus sat at a table with people:

He sat at the table of Matthew, the tax collector, when He called him to be a disciple.

- He sat at the table of Simon, the Pharisee, when the sinful woman anointed His feet with oil.

- He sat at the table of a ruler of the Pharisees, when He healed the man with dropsy on the Sabbath.
- He sat at the table with Mary, Martha, and Lazarus.
- He sat at the table with His disciples, when He instituted the Lord's Supper.
- He sat at the table with the eleven, when He gave them the Great Commission.

Picture, just now, Jesus sitting at a typical rustic table in the little village of Bethany, with those He loves so dearly. I wonder . . . is He sitting on the edge of the chair, leaning forward—intently teaching, explaining, and ministering to those with Him? Or is He "reclining" in the typical Eastern style of dining—sitting but leaning over the table on one elbow? Do you think He is leaning back in His chair, mostly listening—occasionally answering a question sent His way? Does His mind wander somewhat to the difficult times ahead? Are those at Simon's house gathered around, taking it all in—or are they scattered around other parts of the house—maybe picking up bits and pieces of the conversation at the table? Are some of them even outside, enjoying the freshness of the day? Is there a calm in Simon's house this day—everyone relaxing? Or is there a joyful excitement at such a special occasion?—"Jesus has come to Simon's house!" Maybe the uncertainty of these past days has cast an ever-present somber mood over everyone—even Jesus.

We don't know the answers to these questions. But we do know that as Jesus is sitting at the table, a woman comes with an alabaster flask of expensive oil and pours it over the head of Jesus. The reaction of the disciples is quick and indignant—questioning the waste of this costly oil—oil that could have been sold for a significant amount and given to care for the poor. Jesus quickly admonishes the disciples and tells them the anointing is for His burial.

Mark 14:3-8 tells the same story—adding a couple of details:

- *And being in Bethany at the house of Simon the leper, as He sat at the table, a woman came having <u>an alabaster flask of very costly oil of spikenard.</u>*
- *For it might have been sold <u>for more than three hundred denarii</u> and given to the poor.*

Each of the gospels records Jesus being anointed with oil. But how many different anointings are there? Biblical scholars disagree—some say one, some say two. Others say three. All seem to agree, however, that the accounts of Matthew and Mark are the same event. This chart seems to indicate there were three separate anointings:

	Location	Home	Anointed	When
Luke 7:36-50	Galilee/Nain	Simon/Pharisee	Feet	Early Ministry
John 12:1-8	Bethany	Lazarus	Feet	6 days/Passover
Matt. 26:6-13	Bethany	Simon/Leper	Head	2 days/Passover
Mark 14:3-9	Bethany	Simon/Leper	Head	2 days/Passover

To understand what is happening, we must look at Hebrew culture and also the Mosaic Law concerning the selection and preparation of the Passover Lamb. To do so, we have taken the following text from the website inspired2think.wordpress.com.

Understanding the Culture

There is something happening here that is more obvious to Hebrew people than it is to us. In that culture, it was hospitable if you had a guest in your house, to provide water in a bowl for them to wash their feet, as they will have just walked through the dusty byways of Israel. To that water, you would add droplets of perfume to provide a pleasant aroma, but not to be wasteful in the amount that you add because in the Torah you were commanded not to be wasteful.

The rabbis had decided that when you are celebrating someone coming to your house it is okay to use perfume, but it is not okay to use pure nard (spikenard). Why? Because this was seen to be a waste, so if you were wasting resources then you were violating a command of the Torah.

How does Jesus defend both instances? He says that they are not rubbing the pure nard on My feet and pouring it on My head to celebrate Me; they're using pure nard on My feet and head as an act of mourning for My burial. So He defends them by saying this is not an act of celebration and rejoicing. This is an act of mourning, and since it's an act of mourning it fits in with the law.

Choosing the Passover Lamb

Passover lambs were chosen six days in advance. This allowed them to be brought in, often into the family home and inspected for five days. They were inspected to ensure that they were free from blemish, including the legs, ankles, and feet, as they are easily damaged or marked in the rocky hillsides. At this point, they would take the anointing oil and rub it into the ankles and feet, prior to them being inspected for a further 5 days.

So six days before the Passover, Jesus is at someone's house in Bethany and He is anointed for burial by having pure nard rubbed on His feet and ankles. That was His first anointing prior to His crucifixion.

The second anointing happens two days before Passover. The Passover lamb was anointed this second time on their head to announce that they were free from disease or blemish. This is in contrast to the first time, which was on their feet six days before. The head of Jesus was anointed two days before He was crucified and was a sign that He was well, without sickness or defect.

The first Passover lamb anointing was on the feet six days before Passover; the second anointing was on the head two days before, and then the Passover lambs were sacrificed on Passover (which is Nissan 14) from the ninth hour.

We read that following His second anointing, Jesus and the twelve disciples return to Jerusalem from Bethany on the next day, to partake of the Passover meal. This was followed by His arrest, trial and crucifixion the following day when Jesus died around the ninth hour, about 3pm, which was the same afternoon that the Passover lambs were killed.

The anointing of Jesus at Bethany, at the home of Simon the leper, was not just a spur-of-the-moment act. Jesus is going to be the sacrificial lamb, fulfilling all the prophesies of the Messiah. Just as Jesus did His whole life, He would keep the law given by God to the Hebrew people—He is anointed as the sacrificial lamb.

This day is also known as Spy Wednesday. Today will be the day Judas Iscariot decides to betray Jesus. The idea that one of His chosen apostles would abandon and betray His master defies understanding for most of us. It is almost incomprehensible.

For this reason, we have chosen to discuss this sad and difficult subject in chapter eight—a chapter fully given to discussing Judas. We will gather all the information we can find—both from scripture and tradition. We will try to understand what led to this tragedy.

Therefore, here, we will simply provide you with what the gospels say about this day:

- *Then <u>one of the twelve, called Judas Iscariot,</u> went to the chief priests and said, "What are you willing to give me if I deliver Him to you?" And they counted out to him <u>thirty pieces of silver.</u> So from that time he sought opportunity to betray Him* (Matthew 26:14-16).
- *Then Judas Iscariot, one of the twelve, <u>went to the chief priests to betray Him</u> to them. And when they heard it, they were glad, and promised to give him money. <u>So he sought how he might conveniently betray Him</u>* (Mark 14:10-11).
- *<u>Then Satan entered Judas,</u> surnamed Iscariot, who was numbered among the twelve. So he went his way and conferred with the chief priests and captains, how he might betray Him to them. And they were glad, and <u>agreed to give him money.</u> So he promised and sought opportunity to betray Him to them <u>in the absence of the multitude</u>* (Luke 22:3-6).

Silent Wednesday has not been so silent. A betrayal, an evil plot to kill Jesus, and the anointing of Jesus's head—validating Him as the sacrificial lamb for sin—are not insignificant events in the story of these eight days.

And the day of rest for Jesus and His disciples becomes written into history.

LIFE APPLICATION

But each one is tempted when he is drawn away by his own desires and enticed. Then, when desire has conceived, it gives birth to sin; and sin, when it is full-grown, brings forth death (James 1:14-15).

Hate never starts as hate. There is always a progression from the seed of discontent to the mountain of hate. And the path along the way is constantly filled with opportunities to go another way.

The religious leaders' path of conflict with Jesus started with a curiosity toward this unusual Jew. They watched him and listened to Him speak. They saw His miracles, and they were affected by His mere presence—just as the people were.

But their desire for power, privilege, wealth, and notoriety clouded what they were seeing and hearing. Little by little, the seed grew until murder became the desire of their heart.

Question: What are the little seeds of discontent in your heart? And how much have they grown? More importantly, what are you doing to allow the Holy Spirit to remove them and plant the seed of love in their place?

It is so easy to read the story of Jesus's head being anointed at the house of Simon and to find it interesting, but little else. Let us not make that mistake. The fulfillment of prophesy, the validation of His position as the Messiah, and the confirmation that He indeed is the perfect Lamb of God may well be the most important event of Silent Wednesday.

Jesus knew its significance. The disciples—not so much.

Question: As you read the account of Jesus being anointed, did the story begin to have a deeper meaning? Did you begin to see how insignificant the value of the money was and even the caring of the poor in relationship to the confirmation of who Jesus really is? Does it bring you to a deeper worship of Him?

Chapter Seven

> "Jesus gave us a model for the work of the church at the Last Supper... Jesus quietly picked up a towel and basin of water and began to wash their feet."
>
> Phillip Yancey

When the hour had come, He sat down, and the twelve apostles with Him. Then He said to them, "With fervent desire I have desired to eat this Passover with you before I suffer" (Luke 22:14-15).

Passion Week – Day Five
Maundy Thursday

You missed it! If you had planned to walk with Jesus up the hillside to His place of prayer this His last time—you missed it. If you wanted to see His face and attempt to glean a sense of the emotions He is experiencing as another "last time" passes by—you missed it. If you wanted to hear the last conversation between Jesus and His Father from this hillside overlooking Bethany—you missed it.

The sun has risen some time ago, and Jesus is beginning to set the day in order with instructions to His disciples for tonight's Passover meal. Today is Thursday, and Jesus completed His last night of rest just a few hours ago. Never again will He sleep in this mortal body. Sleep will not find the disciples tonight, nor will their heads find rest on a pillow. There will be no returning to Bethany following a long day with Jesus.

The fulfillment of the Promised Messiah is getting so close, and tonight will be a time of confusion, fear, and uncertainty for the disciples. But first, they will celebrate a very special Passover meal. It will become known as The Last Supper or the Lord's Supper:

> *Now on the first day of the Feast of Unleavened Bread the disciples came to Jesus, saying to Him, "Where do You want us to prepare for You to eat the Passover?" And He said, "Go into the city to a certain man, and say to him, 'The Teacher says, "My time is at hand; I will keep the Passover at your house with My disciples."'" So the disciples did as Jesus had directed them; and they prepared the Passover.*
>
> – Matthew 26:17-19

Jerusalem at Passover is not the same as it is the rest of the year. There is an energy that permeates the city. There are noises not found at other times. There are smells drifting throughout the city. Some are the smell of food tempting the senses. Others are the presence of people—lots of them. And the smell of the animals is an inescapable odor that everyone chooses to ignore but can't. There are faces that are new to the city—complete with confusion, amazement, and awe—almost in a trance as they wander around—not sure where they are, where they are going, or what they are supposed to do. The first-timers to the city struggle to adjust to the sounds and the activities surrounding them—like adapting to bright sunlight without sunglasses.

Palm Sunday to Resurrection Sunday

In every corner of the city, plans for Passover are being consummated. The rich have chosen their "perfect" lamb for sacrifice—hoarding it in a protected place and very much pleased with themselves. Their haughty expressions reveal a confidence that their choice lamb will be a pleasing aroma to Yahweh. The preferred locations for a Passover meal have already been taken, and meticulous preparations have started. Elsewhere, the poor have spent their last denarii on a pair of doves or pigeons, praying that Yahweh will be pleased with their sacrifice of a Burnt Offering. As for the Passover lamb, the poor join together, three or four household, to share the cost and to celebrate Passover.

Jerusalem has experienced many Passover feasts in the past, complete with the array of people and the excitement of this most sacred of all Hebrew celebrations. This year's Passover feast is not the first one—but this one is different.

Throughout the city, pockets of conversation have but one topic of discussion—the opinions and stories concerning Jesus. The Sunday procession, the Monday ruckus in the Temple, and the verbal battles on Tuesday have set the city on a curious edge. Who is this Jesus, and why are the priests and scribes so preoccupied with Him?

The stories are getting distorted and exaggerated as they are repeated and embellished. In the middle of it all, the scribes and Pharisees and other religious leaders are scattered about working the crowds—like seasoned politicians—adding a measure of tension and conflict to a division that seems to be growing. Their influence on the people is still strong, and they are using their power to portray Jesus as a blasphemer and a fraud. To most, it started as casual conversation, but now, these words of discourse are fanning the flames of conflict.

Peter and John have just passed through the imposing gates of the city—their brisk journey from Bethany complete. They quickly stomp the dust from their sandals as they step unto the stone streets of Jerusalem and continue steadfastly ahead. The excitement of the city grabs their attention—but only for a brief moment. They are looking for the man with the pitcher:

> *And He sent Peter and John, saying, "Go and prepare the Passover for us, that we may eat." So they said to Him, "Where do You want us to prepare?" And He said to them, "Behold, when you have entered the city, <u>a man will meet you carrying a pitcher of water;</u> follow him into the house which he enters. Then you shall say to the master of the house, <u>'The Teacher says to you</u>, "Where is the guest room where I may eat the Passover with My disciples?"' Then he will show you a large, furnished upper room; there make ready."*
>
> – Luke 22:8-12

The disciples' eyes are rapidly scanning through the crowds as they scurry along. They glance past each vendor post in search of the man with the pitcher. As they wind their way through the crowds, some recognize them as being with Jesus, and they call out to them, "Where is the Teacher?" "Is the Teacher here?" "We came to see the Teacher!" But their only acknowledgement is a quick glance—they have no interest in stopping to engage those calling out.

It seems longer, but it is only a short time and suddenly, they are engaging the man with the pitcher. He is headed home, and Peter and John follow him—just as Jesus instructed.

The walk is not a long one, but it is up the hill on the east side of Mount Zion—just a short distant from the palace of Caiaphas. They enter the courtyard just behind the man and request the master of the house. Upon his arrival, the disciples say to him, *The Teacher says to you*.

Immediately, their purpose for coming is known. With five small words, there will be no questions concerning motives or intent. With five small words, it is as though Peter and John were old friends of the master of the house: *The Teacher says to you*.

This was not the first time Jesus had sent the disciples on a mission this week. The first time was to secure a colt from the man in Bethphage. His triumphal entry into Jerusalem would require a colt of a donkey—so that the prophecy of Zechariah 9:9 may be fulfilled. As Jesus sent them into the village, He said, *And if anyone says anything to you, you shall say, "The Lord has need of them"* (Matthew 21:3b). "The Lord has need of them." Those six words were enough. No more questions were asked—no more resistance was given—no more hesitancy or doubt.

The power and the presence and the person of Jesus captivate people. That was true as He walked on this earth, and it is true today:

- **He is Lord of all.** – *The word which God sent to the children of Israel, preaching peace through Jesus Christ—He is Lord of all* (Acts 10:36).
- **Some call Him Master.** – *And they came to Him and awoke Him, saying, "Master, Master, we are perishing!"* (Luke 8:24a).
- **At the name of Jesus...** – *That at the name of Jesus every knee should bow* (Philippians 2:10a).
- **You call Me Teacher.** – *You call Me Teacher and Lord, and you say well, for so I am* (John 13:13).

Lord, Master, Jesus, or Teacher—the words may be different, but the impact is the same. Jesus has a profound effect on people. Jesus's name makes a difference. Jesus's reputation precedes Him. Jesus demands all the power and authority given to Him by the Father—and now, it is simply: *The Teacher says to you.* But what is it Jesus wants to say to the master of the house? Now that they have his attention and he knows who sent them—what is the message? *Where is the guest room where I may eat the Passover with My disciples?*

Notice, Jesus does not ask for permission to use the room. He does not demand the use of the room. Rather, here is a mutual understanding between Jesus and the master of the house. Jesus knew the heart of the man and his eagerness to be of service to the Teacher.

There is no hesitancy or comments about vacancies or availability. This was the Teacher. That is all that is required. Peter and John are immediately led to a large upper room, and there, they prepare the Passover meal: *So they went and found it just as He said to them, and they prepared the Passover* (Luke 22:13).

The room is prepared. The Passover utensils are in place, the table is set, and the cushions are carefully placed on the floor in front of each setting so that Jesus and the disciples can sit on them and lean with their left arm on the table—thus eating with their right hand, in the traditional Hebrew style of dining—reclining.

There is an energy surrounding the twelve as they arrive with Jesus. There always is as the Passover celebration is at hand. They glance up at the imposing building and then ascend the steps in anticipation—some softly commenting about the building's architecture as they climb upward. The room itself is a large, furnished room—somewhat ornate—capable of making even the wealthy comfortable. The vastness of the room does not overwhelm, and the twelve simply pause and gaze around—absorbing their surroundings—as they enter.

There appear to be no assigned seats, and the disciples scurry to get their choice place—even to the point of disputing who is preferred amongst them. Strangely enough, Judas ends up on the host's (Jesus's) left side—the honored guest's position. John is on Jesus's right, and Peter is across the table from John. Suddenly, this Passover becomes different. It is different because it is different to Jesus.

Matthew and Mark make it appear normal enough:

- *When evening had come He sat down with the twelve* (Matthew 26:20).
- *In the evening He came with the twelve. Now as they sat . . .* (Mark 14:17-18a).

But Luke reveals just how important this Passover is to Jesus: *When the hour had come, He sat down and the twelve with Him. Then He said to them, "<u>With fervent desire I have desired to eat this Passover with you</u> before I suffer, for I say to you, I will no longer eat of it until it is fulfilled in the kingdom of God"* (Luke 22:14-16).

How can we understand the urgency within Jesus? The hour has come. The time is at hand. Surely, His thoughts—as God—and the fulfillment of His perfect plan of redemption flood through His mind and collide with the thoughts and urgency of Jesus—as man—as He feels the time constraint of last-minute teaching, caring, loving, and preparing His chosen apostles.

With fervent desire, Jesus has so looked forward to this Passover meal—His last with His disciples. With fervent desire, Jesus is making this Passover celebration unique—so unique that no other Passover will ever be like it again. With fervent desire, Jesus is modeling humility and servitude. With fervent desire, He is teaching and commanding them on love. And later tomorrow, He will demonstrate that love for the whole world to see—they will never comprehend it, yet they will see it with all its compassion and perfection. John explains it this way: *. . . having loved His own who were in the world, He loved them to the end* (John 13:1b).

The meal begins, and for a moment, normalcy returns. However, the moment is brief. The twelve are settling into the usual rituals of the Feast. The elements are being served—with full explanation of their meaning and significance. In between, the disciples visit quietly. Their conversations are varied as they each privately try to mask the feelings of uneasiness within. They strive to make the abnormal—normal.

Then, without a word, Jesus *rose from supper and laid aside His garments, took a towel and girded Himself. After that He poured water into a basin and began to wash the disciples' feet and wipe them with the towel with which He was girded* (John 13:4-5).

The disciples are stunned into silence. A muffled gasp or two escape the lips. But mostly, there is silence. The shocked mind stifles the tongue. The ability to reason what they are seeing has gone comatose. The question of "How can this be?" goes unanswered, and with all their senses on lockdown, the disciples simply watch Jesus.

One-by-one, Jesus kneels, compassionately and gently washing—then wiping—their feet. Most say nothing—not sure how they should react or feel. How is it the Master is doing the lowest, most humiliating of tasks? It makes the disciples feel uncomfortable—so they simply watch in wonder.

Then He came to Simon Peter (John 13:6a).

By now, Peter has had time to recover. His mind is no longer frozen. His tongue is no longer silent. John 13:6b-9 tells us the rest of the story:

"Lord, are you washing my feet?"

"What I am doing you do not understand now, but you will know after this."

"You shall never wash my feet!"

"If I do not wash you, you have no part with Me."

"Lord, not my feet only, but also my hands and my head!"

With this, Jesus finishes the task, takes His garments, and sits again between Judas and John. Just a few moments ago, as they disputed about the greatest amongst themselves, Jesus had taught them about the least being the first and about he who serves being the greatest. Now, He continues the lesson: *For I have given you an example that you should do as I have done to you. Most assuredly I say to you, a servant is not greater than his master, nor he who is sent greater than he who sent him. If you know these things, blessed are you if you do them* (John 13:15-17).

Jesus is still the Teacher. He is giving those last-minute instructions and lessons. He is the parent with parting words of wisdom: "Keep your coat buttoned"; "Look both ways before crossing"; "Don't talk to strangers." Jesus—with fervent desire—treasures these last minutes and hours with His disciples. Soon enough, He will be telling them to go into the whole world and preach the gospel to every creature. But just now, not a moment shall be wasted. With fervent desire, Jesus teaches His disciples and loves them to the end.

Uneasiness is settling over the disciples. They understand that tonight is different—but without understanding why. Jesus is so at peace and yet so focused—maybe even intense. As they look at each other, the same confusion is on every face—what is going on? Even the looks to Peter and John for understanding yield no explanation. Indeed, this Passover is different. But then the whole week has been excitingly troubling. And the disciples are not yet able to understand the greatness of these eight days of history. They do not understand they are in the midst of the "Greatest Story Ever Told."

Then Jesus, without anger or animosity, softly says, *Assuredly, I say to you, one of you will betray Me* (Matthew 26:21). He looks at no one in particular as the words of truth are delivered with sadness. Just hearing Himself say the words must be bringing sorrow to Jesus. John tells us so: *He was troubled in spirit* (John 13:21). For several moments, the words hang in the air in silence. If a pin had dropped, it would have sounded like an earthquake. Eyes flicker around—but there are no voices or movement.

For the disciples, uneasiness has turned to exceeding sorrow. Shock would not be too harsh a word. Anxiety levels are spiking off the charts, and thoughts of guilt are creeping into their minds. After all, this is the Master—He who knows their thoughts and hearts. Time comes to a screeching halt, and breathing is paused in mid-breath. Horror blankets every face. Their minds are still reeling from Jesus washing their feet—and now this? The disciples are on overload.

Slowly, one by one, the twelve all begin to ask the same question: "Is it I?" "Lord, is it I?" "Is it I?" And John—at the urging of Peter—leans over on Jesus's breast and asks, "Lord, who is it?"

He answered and said to them, "It is one of the twelve, who dips with Me in the dish" (Mark 14:20).

Then Judas, who was betraying Him, answered and said "Rabbi, is it I?" He said to him, you have said it (Matthew 26:25).

And having dipped the bread, He gave it to Judas Iscariot, the son of Simon (John 13:26b).

Having received the piece of bread, he then went out immediately. And it was night (John 13:30).

Judas is gone, but we will see him again soon.

The meal continues—almost as a refuge from the events that are unfolding. Another of the elements is served, explained, and consumed according to the Mosaic Law. The eleven remaining disciples try to converse amongst themselves—but their minds race elsewhere. Jesus is not finished putting His mark on this Passover feast.

The Passover meal includes the consumption of four separate cups of wine. With the meal nearing its conclusion, Jesus takes the third cup, the cup of redemption, and most certainly recites the traditional blessing over the wine: "Blessed are you, LORD our God, King of the universe who creates *the fruit of the vine."* (www.jewishvoice.org)

As the disciples partake with Jesus, Mark tells us Jesus again makes this Passover unique:

> *And as they were eating, Jesus took bread, blessed and broke it, and gave it to them and said, "Take, eat; this is My body." Then He took the cup, and when He had given thanks He gave it to them, and they all drank from it. And He said to them, "This is My blood of <u>the new covenant,</u>*

> *which is shed for many. Assuredly, I say to you, I will no longer drink of the fruit of the vine until that day when I drink it new in the kingdom of God."*
>
> – Mark 14:22-25

Jesus is establishing a new covenant with those who would believe in Him—the promise of forgiveness of sin through His broken body and shed blood. This is the covenant of redemption.

While the covenant is new, the plan of redemption is not. With the fall of man in the Garden of Eden, God had a plan. It was never modified; it was never changed; it was never diluted; it was never given before its appointed time—that time established before the foundations of the earth.

But now, the time of the Promised Messiah has arrived—not as the conqueror of the Romans—but as the Conqueror of sin! *And you shall call His name JESUS, for He will save His people from their sins* (Matthew 1:21b).

Forevermore, bread will be blessed, broken, and eaten as a representative of Christ's broken body. Forevermore, the cup will be taken as it represents the shed blood of Jesus. Forevermore, this new covenant, which the disciples are receiving from Jesus just now, shall be a sacred and special moment—fulfilling Jesus's simple instruction: *Do this in remembrance of Me* (Luke 22:19b).

How do we know what is going through the mind of Jesus's disciples? We can only guess. The excitement of sharing another Passover meal with Jesus is present—but different. Jesus is the same—yet different. The ceremony is very familiar—but different.

The meal has concluded, and they follow tradition by ending the Passover meal with the fourth cup and with singing—singing the Psalms. Tradition tells us the Hebrew people sang Psalm 113 and 114 in the middle of the Passover feast and Psalm 118 at the conclusion of the evening:

> *Oh, give thanks to the LORD, for He is good!*
> *For His mercy endures forever.* – verse #1
>
> *You are my God, and I will praise You;*
> *You are my God, I will exalt You.*

Oh, give thanks to the LORD, for He is good!
For His mercy endures forever. – verses #28-29

It is not hard to imagine that as they sing, Jesus's voice is the most enthusiastic—maybe not the loudest—that would surely be Peter's, right? But Jesus enjoys singing praises to the Father, and undoubtedly, He is so uplifted as He sings, "You are My God, I will exalt You." Jesus, knowing the hour that is at hand, is just now rejoicing and leading His disciples in a song of praise!

What do you think this makeshift choir sounds like? Who are the loudest? Who really loves to sing, and who might be just humming the words? Who is it that thinks they have the best voice? Probably it is those who argued about being the greatest. Is the Father chuckling at the sound (noise) He is hearing and yet so pleased with Jesus and His disciples?

As they all escape with Jesus into a resounding and robust song of praise, all fears, uncertainties, and anxiety are momentarily washed away—replaced with the joy and comfort of praising God.

And who is it that is singing off-key?

Jesus is not finished with the evening in the upper room. Remember, He is still the Teacher, and time is short and precious to Him. The result is what history will call The Farewell Discourse or The Upper Room Discourse. As Jesus speaks, He prepares His disciples for His coming death and departure. He warns them of the hatred and persecutions ahead. He gives them commandments to abide in Him and in His love. Within this farewell discourse are some of the most remarkable and quotable words Jesus has ever spoken—words of comfort—words to challenge and words of promise. Here are a few of them from John, chapter 14:

- *Let not your heart be troubled; you believe in God, believe also in Me* (verse #1).
- *I am the way, the truth, and the life. No one comes to the Father except through Me* (verse #6).
- *Believe Me that I am in the Father and the Father in Me* (verse #11).
- *If you love Me, keep My commandments* (verse #15).
- *Let not your heart be troubled, neither let it be afraid* (verse #27).

And from chapter 15:

- *I am the vine, you are the branches. He who abides in Me, and I in him, bears much fruit; for without Me you can do nothing* (verse #5).
- *Greater love has no one than this, than to lay down one's life for his friends* (verse #13).

And from chapter 16:

- *In the world you will have tribulation; but be of good cheer, I have overcome the world* (verse #33).

Jesus's words have always been a salve to His apostles. Whether in a boat that was sinking or on a mountainside with the hungry multitudes, Jesus gave peace. Jesus is the one who calmed the seas; fed the multitudes; turned the water into wine; and healed the lame, the blind, and deaf. Jesus is the one who heals the heart as well as the body. And He still does today. But then Jesus gave them comfort—the assurance of the Comforter, the Helper, the Spirit of truth—the Holy Spirit: *And I will pray the Father, and He will give you another Helper, that He may abide with you forever, the Spirit of truth, whom the world cannot receive, because it neither sees Him nor knows Him; but you know Him, for He dwells with you and will be in you. I will not leave you orphans; I will come to you* (John 14:16-18).

Finally, Jesus ends the evening in the upper room with prayer:

A prayer for Himself: *I have glorified You on the earth. I have finished the work which You have given Me to do. And now, O Father, glorify Me together with Yourself, with the glory which I had with You before the world was* (John 17:4-5).

A prayer for His disciples: *I do not pray that You should take them out of the world, but that You should keep them from the evil one. They are not of the world, just as I am not of the world. Sanctify them by Your truth. Your word is truth* (John 17:15-17).

A prayer for all believers: *I do not pray for these alone, but also for those who will believe in Me through their word; that they all may* *be one, as You, Father, are in Me, and I in You; that they also may be one in Us, that the world may believe that You sent Me* (John 17:20-21).

And when they had sung a hymn, they went out to the Mount of Olives (Matthew 26:30).

As they clear the gates of the city, the heat of a million breathing bodies, the energy of Jerusalem at Passover, and the suffocating presence of a packed city give way to the briskness of an early Spring night.

It is late as Jesus and the eleven pause for a moment—adjusting to the coolness and the quietness of the evening. Some of the disciples pull their garments more tightly around themselves, while others simply draw in a deep breath of fresh air. The lights of the city are losing their impact, and the stars begin to sparkle and dance in the sky. Nature at night has its own voice—and it is a voice that is not muffled by daylight. Those who choose to listen to night's nature will hear its glorious chatter of praise to its Creator.

None of this is lost on Jesus—but it is not His focus—not now. Neither is reflecting on the Passover meal just completed—nor His revelations to the disciples—nor His final words of teaching and mentoring. Just now, Jesus's spirit is becoming troubled.

They are headed to the Mount of Olives, but they will not go up on the Mount of Olives. If the disciples think they are headed back to Bethany after a long and memorable Passover celebration, they are wrong. They will not leave the city this night. However, right now, they are following Jesus as they proceed through the gates of the city, down through the Kidron Valley, and onto the road that leads to the Mount of Olives, Bethany, and Jericho.

History does not reveal if the journey is a brisk one—with Jesus being resolute and determined to face the next moment. Or is it a slower pace—with all being weary from the long day—and Jesus feeling the burden of what is ahead? We simply do not know.

Crossing the Kidron Valley, where the tomb of Zechariah is, Jesus says to them, *All of you will be made to stumble because of Me this night, for it is written: "I will strike the Shepherd, and the sheep of the flock will be scattered"* (Matthew 26:31). Jesus's quoting the prophet Zechariah does not settle well with His disciples—especially the outspoken Peter. It is not so much that Jesus is quoting the prophet that troubles them. Rather, it is that He is applying that prophecy to this moment. The thought of leaving Jesus is incomprehensible for each of them, and Peter says just that:

Even if all are made to stumble, yet I will not be (Mark 14: 29).

Jesus said to him, "Assuredly, I say to you that today, even this night, before the rooster crows twice, you will deny Me three times" (Mark 14:30).

But he spoke more vehemently, "If I have to die with You, I will not deny You!" And they all said likewise (Mark 14:31).

Peter is overwhelmed by the thought of leaving Jesus. From the first time they met, Peter was a disciple. When Jesus found Peter and Andrew on the shores of Galilee, He said, *Follow Me and I will make you fishers of men* (Matthew 4:19). Then both Matthew and Mark record these words: *They immediately left their nets and followed Him.* Peter was not the hesitant disciple. Peter was not the lukewarm disciple. Peter was the immediate disciple. Peter was the ready disciple, and he loved His Master and he served Him well.

Jesus also loved Peter. Luke gives us insight into that love and compassion as He gives us more of the story that is unfolding this Passover evening:

> *And the Lord said, "Simon, Simon! Indeed, Satan has asked for you, that he may sift you as wheat. But I have prayed for you, that your faith should not fail; and when you have returned to Me, strengthen your brethren." But he said to Him, "Lord, I am ready to go with You, both to prison and to death." Then He said, "I tell you, Peter, the rooster shall not crow this day before you will deny three times that you know Me."*
>
> – Luke 22:31-34

Palm Sunday to Resurrection Sunday

Previously, in the region of Caesarea Philippi, Jesus revealed to His disciples His upcoming death and resurrection. Peter rebuked Jesus, saying, *Far be it from You, Lord; this shall not happen to You!* (Matthew 16:22). Jesus's response to Peter was not gentle: *But He turned and said to Peter, "Get behind Me, Satan! You are an offense to Me, for you are not mindful of the things of God, but the things of men"* (Matthew 16:23).

Jesus was correcting, chastising, and teaching Peter—in love. Proverbs 3:11-12 explains, *My son, do not despise the chastening of the LORD, Nor detest His correction; For whom the LORD loves He corrects, Just as a father the son in whom he delights.*

However, here—here on this eventful night—Jesus is not rebuking or even teaching Peter. Rather, what we see is the compassionate Jesus saying, *I have prayed for you, that your faith would not fail* (Luke 22:32). In a short time, the crimes against Jesus will begin in the Garden. Jesus has a right to be on edge, and He is, indeed, troubled in spirit. But just now, He ministers to Peter with love and compassion.

They arrive at the Garden of Gethsemane.

What is your favorite place? We all have them—those places that have borne the memories and experiences that are special to us. These are the places that harbor the people that we love as well. These favorite places may not be meaningful to others, but they are to us. We always seem to return to them—either in person or in thought.

One of Jesus's favorite places was the area around the northern shores of the Sea of Galilee. This is where much of Jesus's ministry, miracles, and teachings occurred and where He spent much of His time. It was there He found many of the twelve. Jesus loved the area, and Capernaum is called by history the "town of Jesus." Matthew 9:1 says, *So He got into a boat, crossed over, and came to His own city.* That city is Capernaum.

But Jesus has another favorite place as well. It is a place of quiet, a place of solitude, and a place of comfort. It is a place where Jesus chose many times to talk to the Father. He has gone there many times with His disciples. And here is where He so much needs to be on this night. The place is called Gethsemane—the Garden of Gethsemane—its name meaning "oil press." The disciples know the place well, and once again, they follow Jesus into the groves of olive trees—expecting another season of prayer before their return to Bethany. But this will not be any usual time of prayer in the Garden. Jesus instructs His disciples to sit and pray: *When He came to the place, He said to them, "Pray that you may not enter into temptation"* (Luke 22:40).

Jesus takes Peter, James, and John with Him as He moves away from the rest. It is here that a normal evening of prayer becomes an epic prayer of distress: *And He began to be troubled and deeply distressed. Then He said to them, "My soul is exceedingly sorrowful, even to death. Stay here and watch." He went a little farther, and fell on the ground, and prayed that if it were possible, the hour might pass from Him* (Mark 14:33b-35).

We would be wrong to gloss over the magnitude of this moment. Luke says He knelt and prayed—Mark says He fell on the ground and prayed—Matthew says He fell on His face and prayed. The distress of this moment has brought Jesus—the man—to His knees in prayer. He has collapsed prostrate on His face.

Much of Christianity and theological analysis of the events in the garden focus on the failure of the disciples to stay awake—not once—not twice—but three times. They point out their obvious failures when Jesus needed them most. Peter particularly is mentioned because Jesus says to him, *What! Could you not watch with me one hour?* (Matthew 26:40). And Mark records Jesus saying, *Simon, are you sleeping? Could you not watch one hour?* (Mark 14:37).

But this moment is not about the disciples—any of them. It is not about a band of followers failing their leader. They will do that soon enough—but not now. They are all tired. Peter and John have been up since early morning preparing for the Passover feast. And the feast itself has all of them physically and emotionally exhausted. They are tired, and they have fallen asleep!

No, this moment is not about the disciples. It is about Jesus—Jesus, the man, at the point of decision. This moment is so huge that often we miss it. We are preparing our minds for Judas's kiss and Jesus's arrest. We know the story of Peter and Malchus's ear and Jesus restoring it. The fact is the rest of the story gets in the way of the best of the story—Jesus at the point of decision.

Let us regroup our thoughts for a moment. Let us look at a troubled Jesus—a very troubled Jesus. All of His life and ministry has been pointing toward now. When Jesus said in John 14:6, *I am the way, the truth, and the life. No one comes to the Father except through Me*—He was speaking of now. When Peter called Him the Christ and Jesus confirmed it—it was pointing to now. When Jesus said, *I have come that they may have life*—He was speaking of now.

We can plan all our lives for something special or extraordinary or monumental. But until that time is actually at hand—it is only planning and preparing and anticipating. For Jesus, the time has arrived. It is the moment—the epic moment—the dramatic moment—the moment of the final decision. For Jesus, the question to be answered right now in the Garden of Gethsemane—the decision to be made now is: "Will I be obedient to the will of the Father?"

And Jesus is troubled. Look at what scripture tells us of this moment:

- *My soul is exceedingly sorrowful, even to death* (Matthew 26:38).
- *He began to be troubled and deeply distressed* (Mark 14:33).
- *He began to be sorrowful and deeply distressed* (Matthew 26:37).
- *And being in agony, He prayed more earnestly* (Luke 22:44a).
- *His sweat became like great drops of blood falling down to the ground* (Luke 22:44b).
- *An angel appeared to Him from heaven, strengthening Him* (Luke 22:43).

Look at these descriptions, from Strong's Concordance, of the underlined words above: Grieved all around, intensely sad, agitated like roiling water, heavy in mind, anguish, anxiety, conflict, or contention.

Jesus is struggling—big time! Not now nor has there ever been a question of who He is and what His purpose is. But Jesus—the man—is desperately asking for another way. He pleads with the Father, He petitions the Father, and He implores the Father. But He always submits to the Father: *Nevertheless not My will, but Yours, be done* (Luke 22:42b).

Paul tells us in Hebrews 5:7 that the prayers and supplications He is offering up to the Father are with *vehement cries and tears*. Paul continues: *Yet He learned obedience by the things which He suffered*. Obedience to the will of the Father—that is what is before Jesus right now.

However, let us clearly understand—the difficulty is not in the willingness to be obedient—it is in going through with the task at hand. Jesus understood that exact issue when, just moments earlier, He instructed His disciples: *Watch and pray, lest you enter into temptation. The spirit indeed is willing, but the flesh is weak* (Mark 14:38). The issue for Jesus (and us) is not a willing spirit, but a weak flesh. Paul says it is *in the days of His flesh* that Jesus cried out. That is now—at this moment—in the garden. Jesus does not want another mission—He wants another way to complete that mission. Jesus is willing to be the sacrifice, but He desires a path without crucifixion.

William Hendriksen, Professor of New Testament Literature at Calvin Theological Seminary explains: "**Though it will never be possible for our minds to penetrate into the mystery of the horror Jesus experienced in Gethsemane, we cannot be far amiss if we state that it probably included at least this, that He was given a preview of the agonies of the fast approaching crucifixion. He had a foretaste of what it meant to be 'forsaken' by His heavenly Father.**"

Jesus knows what is coming—and He is troubled. Jesus is crying out to the Father. But there is no answer. Jesus pleads, but the Father is silent. He is not going to dictate, influence, or manipulate the decision. He is not going to make a recommendation to Jesus. He is not going to be an advisor or counselor. And Jesus must decide what He will do.

This moment is one of solitude for Jesus. The multitudes are not here. The disciples are in the distance—and now the Father is silent. Jesus is alone with His thoughts—He is alone with His sorrow—He is alone with His agony.

The Father's silence tells Jesus everything. He knows there is no other way but the cross of Calvary. It is a great moment of victory for Jesus. The decision is made. There is no more "Is that your final answer?" This is the epic moment when faith is greater than feared fate!

When the spirit is willing and the flesh is weak, God will send an angel to strengthen us. That is the story of Gethsemane. It is a story of victory. It is a story of submission. It is a story of love. It is the story of an agonizing Jesus being the victorious Jesus.

Palm Sunday to Resurrection Sunday

The three hours of prayer and despair are over, and the quiet Gethsemane—the place of prayer and solitude—suddenly stirs with ill intent. Evil has entered the olive grove in the form of *a great multitude with swords and clubs*. (Mark 14:43) Sent from the chief priests, scribes and Pharisees, John adds the group included *a detachment of troops*. (John 18:3) Leading them was Judas—one of the twelve.

Anxiety and tension immediately explode all around and envelop everyone's emotions. It mattered not whether from surprise, battle ready, or bewilderment, the scene is now toxic—bordering on explosive.

The kiss of betrayal comes quickly: *Greetings, Rabbi!* (Matthew 26:49) says Judas. Jesus replies, *Judas, are you betraying the Son of Man with a kiss?* (Luke 22:48). He does just that, and immediately, the troops take Jesus into custody.

What could have become a battle does not. Jesus does not permit it. The troops are ready for battle; the Jewish leaders are expecting conflict; and Peter pulls his sword and cuts off the ear of Malchus, the servant of the high priest.

But there will be no fight in the garden this day. Jesus says to Peter, *Put your sword in its place, for all who take the sword will perish by the sword. Or do you think that I cannot now pray to My Father, and He will provide Me with more than twelve legions of angels? How then could the Scriptures be fulfilled, that it must happen thus?* (Matthew 26:52-54).

Just a few minutes earlier, Jesus submitted to the Father and confirmed that *it must happen thus*—therefore fulfilling Scripture and the prophets. There will be no swords, clubs, or weapons unleashed this night. Jesus can call ten thousand angels—but He does not. There could be much blood shed tonight—but there will be none. The shedding of blood will come tomorrow on the hill of Golgotha.

With that, Jesus gently replaces and heals the ear of Malchus.

Then all of the disciples forsook Him and fled (Matthew 26:56b).

LIFE APPLICATION

He went a little farther, and fell on the ground, and prayed that if it were possible, the hour might pass from Him. And He said, "Abba, Father, all things are possible for You. Take this cup away from Me; nevertheless, not what I will, but what You will" (Mark 14:35-36).

Jesus's purpose was to save people from their sins. It was the reason He came as the Messiah. It was a commitment He made and understood from a very young age.

But commitment requires action. If Jesus had decided the cost of fulfilling His commitment was too great, then His coming would have only been a hollow promise. But Jesus's commitment was manifested on the cross.

It was in Gethsemane that the commitment became finalized. Submitting your life to Jesus requires finality in purpose and resolve. But it also requires submission. In the end, Jesus submitted. The Father requires it.

Question: Have you totally submitted to God? Is there any situation, you would not totally submit? Maybe separating from a friend who is spiritually toxic for you—or letting go of something that is stunting your spiritual growth—or something taking too much of your time?

There is peace that comes with total submission to the Master. Following His time of agony in the garden, Jesus experienced great peace within—knowing that what was to come was the right thing. It was also the will of the Father.

Question: Have you found that inner peace that comes only when you are completely submitted to the will of God? Jesus had a Gethsemane experience—that time of total submission. Have you had your Gethsemane?

Chapter Eight

> "Judas Iscariot was not a greatly wicked person, just a common money-lover, and like most money-lovers, he did not understand Christ."
>
> Aiden Wilson Tozer

Even my own familiar friend in whom I trusted, who ate my bread, has lifted up his heel against me (Psalm 41:9).

Judas Iscariot
Tragedy in the Midst of Victory

Put away the stones to be cast. You will not need them here. Replace them to their pouch. Remove the pouch and set it aside. Judas Iscariot need not be stoned in the arena of public judgment. He will not be condemned here. He will not be ridiculed here. His decisions and actions speak for themselves, and history has recorded them for eternity. There are no excuses for Judas. His betrayal of the innocent Jesus is appalling and almost unexplainable.

The story of Judas is a tragedy in the midst of the greatest spiritual victory ever—and we weep with sadness. It is a story that need not have happened—yet it did. It is not a story that is highlighted in biblical text—nor is it ignored. Many of its details are left untold. To say Judas, one of the twelve, betrayed Jesus is enough.

Why then are we dedicating an entire chapter of this book to tell his story? Why are we striving to understand what led to this tragedy? Why risk the possibility that we will draw conclusions and opinions which exceed the scope of fact—thus joining the volume of scholars and others who have unwittingly or unfortunately done so before?

The answer is not very complex: In the midst of the story of Judas and his betrayal are lessons for us to learn and ponder. As we look at the tragedy of Judas, let us not think too highly of ourselves.

"Jesus, we ask for Your purified and perfect wisdom as we look at this sad journey of the life of Your disciple Judas Iscariot. The story grieves You, even as Your servant David foretold in Psalm 41. There, You called him Your familiar friend. When he came to betray You in the Garden of Gethsemane, You said, 'Friend, why have you come?' Help us to understand the decisions Judas made along the way that changed his mind and his heart toward You. Amen."

The amount of desired information on the life of Judas Iscariot is extensive; however, the amount of actual information is quite minimal at best. So many questions have been asked that have no answers, and the resulting path has often led to speculation. There is so much we do not know about Judas, his family, or his background.

What then do we know? We know he was the son of Simon Iscariot, but we know nothing about Simon—who he was or what he did. We know his family is most likely from the small town of Kerioth in southern Judea—but even that is not certain.

If he were indeed from Kerioth, he would have been the only one of the twelve apostles not from the Galilean area—thus an "outsider." However, that is not to say he either felt like an outsider or that he was treated like an outsider. Many have attempted to connect those dots in an attempt to explain his actions. That is a large and dangerous step to take—a large "it is possible" on which to make assumptions. We just don't know.

We do know Judas was chosen by Jesus to be one of the twelve. We are not told the circumstances of how or why he arrived from Judea to Galilee. None of the gospels tell us how, where, or when Jesus selected him to be an apostle. Did Judas approach Jesus and ask to be close to Him? Did Jesus point to him in a crowd and call to him? Was he recommended to Jesus by someone else? Probably not. We do know Jesus spent the night in prayer before He chose the twelve: *And it came to pass in those days, that he went out into a mountain to pray, and continued all night in prayer to God. And when it was day, he called unto him his disciples: and of them he chose twelve, whom also he named apostles* (Luke 6:12-13).

The inclusion of Judas was not a spur-of-the-moment decision, nor was it a mistake. Neither was its purpose to make Judas a necessary villain. He was not setup by Jesus to be a failure or simply included amongst the twelve to fulfill biblical prophecy—but fulfill biblical prophecy he did indeed.

His name means "Jehovah leads." That name alone suggests his parents were devout Jews who desired their son would be led by Jehovah and be a devout Jew as well. Judas was probably a zealous young man, but not necessarily outspoken and vocal.

Palestine was a political hotbed during the time of Jesus. It was coveted, not for its land, but for its location. It was the access route from Rome to Egypt. Control of the entire region required control of Palestine—and Rome was in control.

During this time, there also was much attention and anticipation of the coming Messiah. "Messiah-mania" was prevalent and growing. The Jews were looking for the one who would free them from the bondage of the Romans—the one to overthrow the Romans and set up his own throne. This was not just the mindset of many, but also probably the mindset of Judas. Being the typical impatient youth, he wanted the Messiah to come—and to come now!

It was likely the things Jesus was saying and the miracles He was doing attracted Judas to Him. It is probable that Jesus, being "mighty in words and deeds," made a swift and powerful impression on Judas. It is easy to imagine how quickly he—and many others—formed a picture in their mind of how this Jesus would overthrow Roman rule.

Jesus's reputation and notoriety grew rapidly in His early ministry, and Judas Iscariot—somehow, someway—became a part of it. His excitement and joy of being a part of the Messiah's rise to power with the defeat of Rome was surely a time of visualizing and maybe even dreaming of what would soon transpire. Judas possibly even had dreams for himself in a position of importance.

Expectations that are rooted in hopes, dreams, and preconceived actions often bring disillusionment—even bitter disillusionment. The Hebrew nation, down through the ages, had earthly expectations of the Messiah, His coming, and His conquering. God had eternal purposes for the Messiah—one of freedom from spiritual bondage and one of eternal life. These conflicting purposes led many to turn away from Jesus—even spiritual leaders.

John tells us when Jesus was teaching in the synagogue in Capernaum that His teaching troubled many followers. Jesus said, *I am the bread of life* (John 6:35b), and *I am the living bread which came down from heaven. If anyone eats of this bread, he will live forever* (John 6:51a), and *Whoever eats My flesh and drinks My blood has eternal life, and I will raise him up at the last day* (John 6:54).

Then we read, *Therefore many of His disciples, when they heard this, said, "This is a hard saying; who can understand it?"* (John 6:60). And John continues: *From that time, many of His disciples went back and walked with Him no more* (John 6:66).

It is likely that Judas Iscariot struggled with these very words that Jesus spoke. He was not one of the disciples to walk away from Jesus at Capernaum at this time. However, it is likely his enthusiasm over Jesus was waning.

Who's Who in the Bible by Comay and Browningg says: **"Judas, more than others perhaps, seems to have misunderstood or disregarded Jesus' interpretation of His own Messiahship. Faced with a slow and steady process of disillusionment and disappointment, at what so many of Jesus' followers considered to be lost opportunities (John says they wanted to make him King), Judas's impatience seems to have grown . . ."**

A.W. Tozer says Judas did not understand Christ. This appears to be true. But how could that be? Judas was there for all of Jesus's miracles. Judas was there as Jesus consistently and continually taught and explained His coming and fulfillment as the Messiah. His lessons of living and life and obedience were clear. His teaching on servitude, humility, and love were to the point and often explained with parables.

But the teachings of Jesus were not what drew Judas to Him. Judas was looking for the Messiah to come in all power and authority—to overthrow Rome. But this Messiah (Jesus) was not the messiah of Judas's dreams and expectations.

It appears Judas began to follow a slow, yet sure, path of doubt almost from the beginning. He could not understand nor subscribe to the ministry of Jesus. While still hearing Jesus, he apparently could never accept what he was hearing. His own ideals, beliefs, and expectations blocked his ability to understand Jesus. And almost daily, the disillusionment and disdain was growing in the heart and the mind of Judas.

Let us be clear about the freedom of choice Judas enjoyed. His fulfillment of biblical prophecy, his inclusion as one of the twelve, his decisions that led to his heinous betrayal of Jesus and his ultimate fate were not predetermined for him by prophecy or the requirement that Jesus be betrayed by Judas Iscariot or Calvary would not have occurred.

Every step in the life of Judas Iscariot was taken by Judas alone. Judas alone decided what he would believe and whom he would believe. Just like you and me, Judas—regardless of the influence or pressures from others, whether human or demonic—made his own decisions. And with each decision, he and he alone bore the consequences of those decisions.

There is often confusion concerning biblical prophecy and its fulfillment. That is especially true as we look at the life of Judas Iscariot. Did Judas have to betray Jesus in order to fulfill prophecy? What if in the middle of Jesus's teaching, one day the light came on in Judas's heart and he changed his mind and began to truly believe in Jesus? And what if, at that moment, he confessed his thoughts of betrayal to Jesus and repented? What about prophecy then?

Judas's actions were not predetermined; they were pre-known. *For Jesus knew from the beginning who they were who did not believe, and who would betray Him* (John 6:64b). Biblical prophecy is true because God has the foreknowledge of everything that will ever happen. Biblical prophecy is not a guess or a prediction. Rather, it is a statement of truth of what will come to pass. If Judas had changed his mind, then biblical prophecy would have foretold the story of someone else or some other event—not the story of Judas Iscariot—the one who would betray Jesus. But Judas did not repent, and Judas did not change his mind. And Psalm 41:9 is fulfilled prophecy because of the choices made by Judas. What a sad and unnecessary story.

Finally, on this subject, many believe Judas's betrayal was required because it allowed the chief priests to identify Jesus and thus capture Him. Hence, were there no betrayal, there would have been no arrest, nor trial, nor crucifixion. John tells us otherwise:

> *Then Judas, having received a detachment of troops, and officers from the chief priests and Pharisees, came there with lanterns, torches, and weapons. <u>Jesus therefore,</u> knowing all things that would come upon Him, <u>went forward and said to them,</u> "Whom are you seeking?" They answered Him, "Jesus of Nazareth." <u>Jesus said to them, "I am He."</u> And Judas, who betrayed Him, also stood with them.*

– John 18:3-5

If there had not been a kiss of betrayal by Judas, Jesus would not have escaped via a back path out of Gethsemane and free from the detachment of troops. No, quite the opposite occurred—Jesus "went forward." Jesus asked, "Who are you seeking?" Jesus replied to them, "I am He."

Jesus was going to the cross, and His fulfillment as the Messiah was not dependent on a spiritually sick and delusional Judas. Nonetheless, Judas did willfully and tragically place the kiss of betrayal on the cheek of Jesus.

Some would paint Judas Iscariot as a demonic and evil person from the start. These people will point to John's harsh words of Judas and define him as simply the bad apple—the one with no hope of redemption and no desires but for evil. They will say Judas was a thief and a fraud long before his life with Jesus. They will say, from the start, he was deceptive, cunning, calculating, and deceitful.

While this may be true or partially true, we do know that Judas's love of money was a flaw for certain. John points that out in John 12:6: *This he said, not that he cared for the poor, but because he was a thief, and had the money box; and he used to take what was put in it.* Judas's love of money is established here by John, and the result was Judas was a thief. However, as we study scripture, we find silence concerning the character of Judas up until just six days before the Feast of Unleavened Bread. The lone exception is found in John 6:70-71. It is the time discussed earlier where Jesus's teaching in Capernaum confused many and they left Him.

At the conclusion, we read, *Jesus answered them, "Did I not choose you, the twelve, and <u>one of you is a devil?</u>" He spoke of Judas Iscariot, the son of Simon, for it was he who would betray Him, being one of the twelve.*

The harsh words from Jesus, calling one of His twelve a devil, must be looked at in its context. According to Strong's Concordance, there are two key words that are translated "devil." The first is *daimonion*, and its meaning is "a demonic being" or "supernatural spirit." We see this word used when Jesus heals the boy with a demonic spirit that seized him: *And as he was still coming, <u>the devil</u> threw him down, and tare him. And Jesus rebuked the unclean spirit, and healed the child, and delivered him again to his father* (Luke 9:42, KJV). Interestingly, the NKJV and many other translations use the word "demon" in this verse, instead of the word "devil." It matters not—the meanings are the same. Here, "devil" refers to a demonic being or spirit.

The second word in the Greek that is translated as "devil" is *dialolos*, and its meaning is "a traducer" or "false accuser" or "slanderer." This is the word Jesus used to describe Judas in John, chapter six. Jesus was not calling Judas a demonic being, but rather a slanderer or traducer. If Judas Iscariot were under strong demonic control or influence at this time, surely, he would have exhibited behavior that would have drawn the attention of the gospel writers. There seemingly were no red flags of behavior from Judas until near the very end.

Judas Iscariot's life is not that rare anomaly of sin gone wild. It is not a story of radical and demonic destruction—wreaking havoc throughout the land—from beginning to tragic end. It is not the atomic bomb of evil, seeking to level all and everything in its path. However, the life of Judas may be Satan's poster child of how to conquer and destroy a life.

The ruin of Judas was a sure and steady decline. His life was filled with decisions that would shape his thoughts and his actions. At every step, Judas had a choice, and with each decision, sin was an option.

What started as a dream of a rescuing Messiah, complete with all the strategies and details required, soon became tainted with questions and doubt. Grains of uncertainties entered, then doubt. Disappointment would come, followed by disillusionment and disdain. Disdain bred anger, and anger led to action. And the fall of Judas was complete.

The tragedy of Judas Iscariot is imbedded in the reality that with every choice he made, opportunity to change was an option as well. Sadly, Judas could not escape the vision of "his" messiah. He could not see the Messiah of Jesus. He could not believe in the Savior of his soul.

Judas had no interest in servitude or sacrifice and suffering. He didn't want this Messiah or this Mentor or this Master. Judas simply chose not to understand Jesus, and the separation and the gulf that was building between them grew—steadily and continually.

Paul warned Timothy about the tragedy of loving money: *For the love of money is the root of all kinds of evil, for which some have strayed from the faith in their greediness, and pierced themselves through with many sorrows* (1 Timothy 6:10). This was a fatal flaw for Judas.

Jesus knew what was happening in the heart of Judas. Yet He loved him just the same. He still taught Judas—as He did the others. He still called him friend—not in deception but because He considered him a friend. Jesus still washed his feet in humbleness and love. It is a tremendous picture of agape love lived out.

Gethsemane became the place of decision for Jesus. We looked at that closely in the previous chapter. It was in Gethsemane where Jesus prayed in agony, much sorrow, and distress. It was there He pleaded for another way, asking that this cup be taken from Him. It was in the Garden that Jesus accepted—yes, even embraced—the will of the Father. It was there Jesus committed to the cross of Calvary.

Just as surely, somewhere within the last days of his life, Judas made the final decision to betray Jesus. Somewhere, he committed his feelings to action. Somewhere, he rejected Jesus with a decisive heart and the doors of his heart swung open wide for Satan. We read in Luke 22:3-4, *Then Satan entered Judas, surnamed Iscariot, who was numbered among the twelve. So he went his way and conferred with the chief priests and captains, how he might betray Him to them.* This was just before Judas went to the chief priests and settled for his betrayal fee.

The second time was at the Last Supper, right after Jesus dipped the bread and gave it to Judas: *Now after the piece of bread, Satan entered him. Then Jesus said to him, "What you do, do quickly"* (John 13:27).

At this point, it would be futile to reason out Judas's thought and purposes. Satan was his master, and sin was his mission. Reasoning power was vacant. Logical thinking was lost. Judas's choices made him a prisoner, and his mind was surely in turmoil. It has been said that **"sin makes us stupid."** This certainly applies to Judas. It has also been said that **"sin will take you farther than you want to go, keep you longer than you want to stay, and cost you more than you want to pay."** This too applies to Judas.

Later on, we learn, *Then Judas, His betrayer, seeing that He had been condemned, was remorseful and brought back the thirty pieces of silver to the chief priests and elders* (Matthew 27:3). Different translations use different words: "was remorseful," "repented himself," "was seized with remorse," "felt remorse." Strong's Concordance tells us the word means: to care afterwards, regret, repent (self). Judas was sorry for what he had done. But he never asked for forgiveness from the One he betrayed. He could have, and Jesus surely would have forgiven him—but he didn't.

Judas hung himself and missed the greatest miracles that lay just ahead. He missed witnessing the forgiveness of the thief on the cross. If he had seen that event, maybe he would have been able to find the faith to ask for forgiveness also. But he was not there.

Judas was not there when they found the tomb empty and missed the miracle of a resurrected Jesus. Judas was not there when Jesus appeared to the apostles and they saw Him and talked to Him and were reassured. Judas was not there when Jesus comforted them, gave them final instructions to change the world, and he was not there to see Jesus ascend to the Father. Sin had cost Judas so much more than he wanted to pay.

LIFE APPLICATION

You therefore, beloved, since you know this beforehand, beware lest you also fall from your own steadfastness, being led away with the error of the wicked (2 Peter 3:17).

Choice is movement, and even small steps can become significant. Just watch how quickly an infant can get away from you with their tiny steps. Pastor Rick Nerud has said, "We move a step closer to or further from Christ with each decision we make." And it is amazing how quickly we can wander from His care and protection. Judas did just that.

Question: Peter warns us of falling from our own steadfastness. What little, seemingly insignificant, steps are you taking away from Jesus? What change in attitude and purpose do you need to make that will enable you to turn back to Him?

Judas's faith in Jesus failed him because he didn't understand who Jesus was. Failing to understand the loving and compassionate Jesus prevented Judas from asking for forgiveness. Many people don't believe Jesus can or will forgive them for their terrible acts of sin—and hence, they never ask. Is that you?

Question: What are you too ashamed of to ask Jesus to forgive you? Pray for the faith to ask. It is that simple. Jesus wants nothing more than to bring you to himself, but you must ask.

All of us, as Christians, wander at times. While straight and narrow is the path, our trek is anything but so. Oh, we have occasions of walking close to Jesus, but then we look around and wobble or stumble. Our infant steps lead us into the briars and the brambles—scratching and cutting us spiritually.

Question: Where are you walking today—close by Jesus or in the weeds? What action are you going to take to get closer to Jesus today?

Chapter Nine

> "The marvel of heaven and earth, of time and eternity, is the atoning death of Jesus Christ. This is the mystery that brings more glory to God than all creation."
>
> C.H. Spurgeon

But He was wounded for our transgressions, He was bruised for our iniquities; the chastisement for our peace was upon Him, and by His stripes we are healed (Isaiah 53:5).

Passion Week – Day Six
Good Friday

This is the day! Eternity has it circled on its calendar. The Father has selected it and ordained it. Jesus, the Son, has consented to the events of this day, and Jesus, the man, has submitted to His fate and calling.

When the ninth hour (3:00 p.m.) arrives, Jesus will fulfill the purpose of the Messiah: *And at the ninth hour Jesus cried out with a loud voice, saying, "Eloi, Eloi, lama sabachthani?" which is translated, "My God, My God, why have You forsaken Me?"* (Mark 15:34).

And when Jesus had cried out with a loud voice, He said, "Father, into Your hands I commit My spirit" Having said this, He breathed His last (Luke 23:46).

This is Friday—Good Friday. It is a day that is almost unexplainable, and comprehension struggles in its wake. It is a day that has no peer on the canvass of time. It is a day where the deed of redemption, once completed, will offer hope where hope is absent.

Man has striven to bring this day to life on the big screens of cinema. Writers have exhausted their skill with descriptive and expressive words in volumes of books. Christians have grappled with the horror of the day and yet the joy of Christ's victory. This day, with its meaning and purpose, exhausts one's thoughts and emotions. Yet when the day is over, all of the pieces of this sacred masterpiece will not yet be in place—thus leaving the disciples and everyone else confused and bewildered. *He is risen!* is yet to be exclaimed.

The day will end with emotions spent and minds reeling and confused. Hearts will be broken, and tears will be cascading down faces. Fears will bludgeon the fragile faith of Jesus's faithful, and today will conclude with more questions than answers. Jerusalem will be reeling from the day's events—some so spectacular and dramatic that reports of them will be dismissed as untrue. At the end of the day, Jesus will lay in a tomb, the religious leaders will claim victory, Judas will be dead from guilt—hanged in suicide—the people will be left wondering, and the eleven apostles will be scattered—yet to be brought back to Jesus's side.

But there is a lot to happen before we reach the ninth hour.

Gethsemane is a place of quiet and solitude. It is accented with winding paths and silent olive trees that only speak when the wind gently rustles their sturdy leaves. Gethsemane is not a place where children play. It is a place where souls come to meditate and to think. It is a place where life meets quiet—where thoughts can be sorted, unimpeded by daily clutter. People come here because it is a garden—the Garden of Gethsemane.

Jesus comes here to pray. It is a familiar place to Him and His disciples. Their visits to this place of prayer have been frequent, and for Jesus, this is a special place that provides salve to His soul. On this night, Jesus is in intense prayer, for tonight is a night of decision for Jesus.

But as yesterday becomes today—in the early hours—complete with its chill and darkness—Gethsemane is being disturbed. Its silent serenity has been shattered with the sounds of tense voices and pounding feet on the march. The sight of lanterns piercing the darkness with dancing light and menacing shadows adds an ominous feel to the moment—a disruption to Gethsemane's gentle spirit.

The high priests and scribes, the detachment of troops, and the entourage of religious leaders—all battle ready—have shattered the silence of disciples sleeping against an olive tree. Tension and surprise have replaced a tranquil refuge.

Judas has come. The movement of Roman soldiers overwhelms the silence of the night, and the entourage of religious leaders, sent from the high priest and the Sanhedrin, move with a defiant swagger. They have come to arrest Jesus. The sinister plan of a counterfeit kiss of respect is being implemented, and the Roman soldiers are ready to subdue and capture Jesus. It is He they have come to arrest, and they are anxious to complete the task. Their sheer numbers give them the confidence they will be successful.

However, if one were expecting a battle—ripe with swords, clubs, and other weapons—they would be mistaken. Violence will not visit Gethsemane on this night. There is no resistance from Jesus or His followers—but for the wayward sword of Peter.

The kiss of betrayal is over. The ear, removed by the sword of Peter, has been replaced by the healing touch of the Master. The keg of violence, ready to erupt, has been defused by the gentle voice of Jesus:

> *But Jesus answered and said, "Permit even this." And He touched his ear and healed him. Then Jesus said to the chief priests, captains of the temple, and the elders who had come to Him, "Have you come out, as against a robber, with swords and clubs? When I was with you*

Palm Sunday to Resurrection Sunday

> *daily in the temple, you did not try to seize Me. <u>But this is your hour, and the power of darkness</u>.*"

– Luke 22: 51-53

But this is your hour, and the power of darkness. With these words, Jesus tells us the journey of the sacrificial Lamb of God—the Messiah—has started. The punishment of Jesus is beginning to be meted out. The redemptive price of sin is being paid, and its relentless fury will not subside until Jesus completes His purpose with the words on the cross: *It is finished* (John 19:30).

The disciples have left—all of them, even Peter. The gospel writers are clear on that: *Then <u>all</u> the disciples forsook Him and fled* (Matthew 26:56b). Jesus is alone with His captors—bursting with their bitter anger and hatred. Jesus's words of surrender, *But the scriptures must be fulfilled* (Mark 14:49b), have done nothing to calm the emotions within the priests and scribes. Their gathering hate for Jesus is boiling over, and finally, they believe they have the upper hand. The handling of Jesus is anything but gentle. Matthew Henry describes it thus: **"They hurried him away with violence, as if he had been the worst and vilest of malefactors."**

Within the coming hours, He will be beaten, spit upon, and scourged. Blood will stream down His face from the crown of thorns, and the pain and fatigue of suffering will cause His knees to buckle on the Via Delarosa. Seemingly the whole world will turn against Him. But just now, Jesus is bound and led away to the house of Annas, the former high priest.

It is early in the morning. Light is still hours away. The night air is but a whisper, and yet all feel its chill as they pull their garments tightly around themselves. The arresting troops are briskly moving toward Jerusalem with their prisoner, and as they move away, their sound fades into the darkness. Gethsemane returns to a place of quiet and solitude.

The trek from Gethsemane is not a pleasant walk for Jesus. His hands are bound, and He is handled roughly as they move along. He is taunted and ridiculed by the soldiers and Jewish leaders, as they become bolder and more defiant with each step. The familiar path, often a source of enjoyment for Jesus, has become a laborious journey.

There are no recorded words from Jesus on this road to Annas's house. He is silent—alone with His thoughts and His pain. He is left to bear the abuse with no one there to even offer a glance of understanding. There are no disciples milling around Him. There is no Peter to be brave and brash. There are no admiring multitudes for Him to gaze upon. Only His adversaries are near—but for one. At His side is the Father, and Jesus continues in conversation with Him as they move along, praying for strength—and surely for His captors.

Their movement is purposeful, but not silent, as they march toward the Upper City of Jerusalem, where the wealthy reside and where the Chief Priests and Jewish leaders have their palatial compounds. The commotion of this large arresting group is drawing the curious from their homes and the byways. Their numbers are not large, but nonetheless, the religious leaders do not appreciate their presence, and the priests let their displeasure be known. The curious keep a safe distance but don't go away. There is too much electricity in the air for that. Their journey will end at the walls of the compound. There, the palace guards and the soldiers will turn them away. But just now, they talk amongst themselves, sharing facts and fiction but not overly concerned with separating the two. All the while, they intensely absorb the scene before them. "Who are they arresting?" "Why so many soldiers?" "They all seem to be angry?" "Could it be the one they call Jesus?" The questions come and are answered with replies disguised as fact—all randomly offered from within the group of curious followers. It takes a while, but the consensus soon comes: "Yes, it is the Teacher."

Author's Notes

The challenges and complexities of language translation occasionally lead the translators to a dead-end. The desired word-for-word translation is left void when the receiving language has no path of translation from a more deep and complex language. The Greek language is very deep and complex. It has moods (indicative, imperative, subjunctive, and optative); tenses; voices (active, passive, and middle); and singular, dual, and plural genders—each in masculine, feminine, or neuter. And then there are the Greek accents (acute, grave, and circumflex) within the written language. This is all in addition to breathing—rough breathing or smooth breathing and coronis, which is a mixing of breathing. All of this complexity in the written word makes translating a challenge.

A second challenge to ancient writing translations is chronological accuracy. This is a major issue to the Western world—particularly America. However, in many—if not most—parts of the world, timing sequence is not important. The Western world cares as much about when it happened as what happened. We want to know step by step the process—what happened first, second, or third. We become easily confused when the writer chronologically jumps back and forth in the text. We sort things chronologically, and sequential events are important to us.

However, for much of the world, even today, the only important factor is what happened. The event is more important than when the event happened. That it happened is what is valued. This can be troublesome when translating into English. When translating in a word-for-word translation, rather than a thought-for-thought translation, following chronological sequencing is difficult.

As we examine the events on this day (Good Friday), understanding the sequence of the text has resulted in much discussion and disagreement on what happens next in our story. The gospel of John is not a synoptic gospel, and John is notorious for ignoring the chronological process. In addition, the Greek language leaves the reader struggling for the proper sequence of events:

- John is the only gospel writer who mentions Jesus was taken first to the house of Annas.
- There is confusion concerning Peter's denial of Jesus. Was his first denial at the house of Annas, while his second and third denials were at the palace of Caiaphas? Or were all three at Annas's house? Or were all three at Caiaphas's palace?

- The questioning of Jesus in John 18:12-24—was it by Annas or was it by Caiaphas?
- When did Annas send Jesus to Caiaphas? (John 18:24).

It is with verse 24 of John, chapter 18, that the Greek language leaves the English language with no viable translation. Many scholars believe the verse should read, *Then Annas **had** sent Him bound to Caiaphas, the high priest*. That is precisely what the King James Version reads, whereas the New King James and others omit the word *"had."*

At this point, I would refer you to Matthew Henry's commentary on John, chapter 18. It is a lengthy, yet thorough (and I believe accurate), explanation of this portion of scripture. In his commentary, Henry suggests, for chronological clarity, verse 24 would fit better following verse 13. Hence, all that follows verse 13 occurs at the palace of Caiaphas and thus is more easily aligned with the three synoptic gospels.

For our purposes, we will follow this line of reasoning—while fully aware others may disagree with this theology. Regardless of the chronology, we are certain Peter denied Jesus three times. The events are what matter, and we will stay true to them.

To understand the importance of Jesus's brief encounter with Annas, we must know a little bit about the man. Annas became High Priest in 6 AD but was removed in 15 AD by Valerius Gratus, the procurator of Judea, because Annas was executing people for religious infractions—a practice forbidden by Roman law. The current High Priest is Caiaphas, the son-in-law of Annas. Although the Roman authorities appointed others to the high priesthood, the Jewish people considered Annas to be the high priest by divine law. Thus, he had authority over spiritual matters.

The International Standard Bible Encyclopedia states in its article on Annas, **"Caiaphas, indeed, as actual high priest, was the nominal head of the Sanhedrin which condemned Jesus, but the aged Annas was the ruling spirit."**

"The ruling spirit"—indeed! Annas was a wealthy and powerful man— maybe the wealthiest in all Judea. He controlled the Temple trade and maintained a powerful political influence. He and his family became rich by selling the goods needed by the people for sacrifice in the Temple at outrageous prices—nothing short of extortion. Their notorious "Booths of the sons of Annas" on the Mount of Olives, four market stalls, were a major source of wealth. In his book, *The Life and Times of Jesus the Messiah,* Alford Edersheim says, **"The House of Annas was cursed in the Talmud as 'wealthy, unscrupulous and corrupt leaders of the priesthood whose presence defiled the sanctuary.'"**

Annas's issues with Jesus grew throughout the Lord's ministry. However, when Jesus drove the moneychangers out of the temple a few days ago, the financial impact on Annas and his family was huge. E.G. Lewis comments, **"He raised their ire by striking at the source of their wealth and like a typical Mafia chieftain, Annas responded with violence."** Jesus's actions shut down their operations briefly, thus cutting severely into their bottom line. Holy days, like Passover, were the most lucrative times of the year. After He overturned the tables, the scribes and the chief priests sought to destroy Him (Mark 11:18).

As the curious watch, the large entourage reaches the stopping place at Annas's house. The troops are sent back to their Roman posts, no longer needed nor wanted. The least amount of eye witnesses the better. Jesus, still being tormented, is brought before Annas. He will not be questioned here. He will not be detained here but for a brief moment. Why, then, is He even here?

The fact that Jesus is brought here first speaks to the power and influence of Annas. He may have instructed it. It may be his house is on the way and merely a stopping place along the route to Caiaphas's palace—a place to rest and a place to shed the Roman soldiers. Regardless, Annas wants to look upon the face of "his" prisoner Jesus. He wants to see Him squirm in discomfort and pain. He wants to see the fruit of the successful capture of the One he has come to hate so much. He wants to experience "to the victor be the spoils."

Suddenly, Jesus is standing before Annas—and Annas is savoring the moment. The old man with so much power and influence, just now, feels powerful and mighty. Standing before him is an exhausted and beaten man—just the scene he has pictured and relished in his mind. But Jesus is more than just weary from a long day—He is physically spent.

However, Annas does not see a broken man standing before him. Jesus is weary and worn, but He is not broken. There is a strength within Jesus without explanation. Defeat is not on His face. Despair is not on His countenance, and Annas sees it. Suddenly, the euphoria he is delighting in is drained from his face, and his spirit immediately sinks. Despite the chains that bind Him, Jesus is not the prisoner. He is not enslaved and overcome by the enemy—at least not in spirit. He is not the defeated. He is the Messiah, and by this day's end, He will be the Savior of the world. He is the willing Lamb of God, who is giving His life as a ransom for many: *No one takes it from Me, but I lay it down of Myself. I have power to lay it down, and I have power to take it again. This command I have received from My Father* (John 10:18).

Annas is a troubled man. Still fresh in his mind are the memories of tables overturning, wares being scattered, and coins tumbling to the ground. Revenue losses have long since been tallied, and the amount is large. Deep within the heart of Annas, hate has snatched control from reason. Looking into the eyes of Jesus has brought him no joy, and he turns away with a heart filled with turmoil. The stay at the house of Annas has ended.

Jesus is led away. They are taking Him to Caiaphas and the Sanhedrin for trial. The journey to Caiaphas's palace is short and uneventful—if, indeed, the procession of a bound prisoner and His host of captors can be uneventful. The curious are back with their unconfirmed stories of what happened at Annas's house, and somewhere buried in their midst are Peter and John—far from recovered from the horror and fear of the events in Gethsemane. They are following, wanting to see what will happen to Jesus but not wanting to be recognized or to become part of the story. They are still fearful. John tells us, *And Simon Peter followed Jesus, and so did another disciple. Now that disciple was known to the high priest, and went with Jesus into the courtyard of the high priest. But Peter stood at the door outside. Then the other disciple, who was known to the high priest, went out and spoke to her who kept the door, and brought Peter in* (John 18:15-16).

Things are happening way too fast for the normally reactionary Peter. Always one to respond quickly and with conviction, Peter's mind is numbed by the magnitude of each moment as it unfolds. Seeing Jesus bound and beaten is too much for Peter to process—his heart and mind are reeling. Confusion and fear grip his entire being, and the darkness of the night only adds to his trepidation. Maybe he would be doing better if all this were happening in the light of day—a bright sunny day! But now, in the darkness, Peter is not doing well—not at all!

With John, he enters the courtyard where they have brought Jesus. But Peter is not following close to Jesus's side, as he usually did throughout the past three years. Luke tells us, *But Peter followed at a distance* (Luke 22:54b). John has left him alone in the crowd, and Peter is uneasy. He anxiously looks about, trying to gauge the level of danger, looking about for signs of trouble. His steps are uncertain as he slowly eases into the courtyard and blends with the crowds drifting about.

The courtyard is a flurry of activity, and the night air is vibrating with tension. Servants and palace workers, along with scribes and priests, are moving about—some scurrying to fulfill instructions, others milling about in wait. There is an uncertainty that has enveloped the entire courtyard, and it is adding to the excitement and anticipation. "They have arrested the Teacher!" "What will happen to Him?" "I heard they want to kill Him!" The rumors are bouncing around the courtyard with little validity—just as they were among the curious outside earlier. *What will happen to Jesus, indeed?* Peter wonders and worries.

A fire has been built to combat the early morning cold, and its flickering lights are dancing off the building walls with an eerie overtone. Its warm embers streak up into the night, attracting an ever-increasing number of people. Peter is among them. He finds a place to sit, absorbing some of the fire's warmth, but not sitting so close to be noticed. Peter does not want to be recognized—things are too explosive at this moment.

Those around the fire and those moving about the lower courtyard are keeping an eye on the courtyard above where they have taken Jesus. The open window overhead yields the muffled sounds of what is being said—some audible—but most are not. Mingled with the noise below, the words are mostly lost—even the frequent shouts of anger and the soft but ever-present moans of pain.

The movement through the window above gives fleeting glimpses of the key players. The chief priest is spotted as he moves back and forth in agitation. Guards with weapons are seen. An occasional scribe comes into view. And Jesus, beaten and worn, has been seen as well. Peter catches a glimpse of his Master. His heart sinks, and the picture, arrested in his mind, is doing nothing to ease his fears.

Captured in such a scene of uncertainty, Peter is doing the unthinkable. As Jesus declared to him hours ago in the upper room, Peter is denying he is a disciple of the man from Galilee. His fear produces three denials—two have already occurred, and now, the third comes to life as he sits around the fire.

Luke tells us:

> *Then after about an hour had passed, another confidently affirmed, saying, "Surely this fellow also was with Him, for he is a Galilean." But Peter said, "Man, I do not know what you are saying!" Immediately, while he was still speaking, the rooster crowed. And the Lord turned and looked at Peter. Then Peter remembered the word of the Lord, how He had said to him, "Before the rooster crows, you will deny Me three times." So Peter went out and wept bitterly.*
>
> – Luke 22:59-62

Matthew and Mark declare these words of denial are much stronger and more emphatic than before: *Then He began to curse and swear, "I do not know the Man of whom you speak"* (Mark 14:71). This third time is not a gentle "No, you are mistaken." This is not as he declared earlier, *I neither know nor understand what you are saying* (Mark 14:68b). The gospel writers want to be clear—Peter is denying Jesus, thus fulfilling what Jesus had foretold.

This is the worst moment of the worst day of Peter's life. Never again will Peter be so sorry for his actions. Never again will he feel the pain of turning away from his Master—the One he will later willingly die for. Peter will become a leader of the followers of Jesus. He will preach and declare Jesus to the world and perform miracles under the guidance of the Holy Spirit. Peter will indeed become the faithful follower of Jesus that he envisioned himself to be. But at this moment, on this day, Peter is a broken man.

However, in the midst of Peter's nightmare, his cloud finds a silver lining: *And the Lord turns and looked at Peter* (Luke 22:61a). In an amazing display of love and compassion, Jesus briefly pushes the pause button on all that is happening before Him and to Him. The pain and suffering is halted. The anger and attacks that rage around Him are imprisoned—paused against their will. The ranting of Caiaphas becomes irrelevant. Jesus turns and looks into the eyes of Peter.

This is not the look of "I told you so," nor is it the look of condemnation. It is not a look of disappointment. It is not a look to punish Peter either. Rather, it is a look of love and compassion and a look of understanding for the pain Peter is feeling right now. Though so very brief, it is a look that will bind the Teacher and His student forever. It is a look that will, in the coming days, increase Peter's faith. However, now the pain and guilt is deep, and Peter goes out—away from the fire and away from the people—and weeps bitterly.

The look of love on the face of Jesus will be a salve for Peter's guilt. Peter will replay all the pride and brashness of past comments and action. These are the memories that now humble and embarrass him. There will be much regret and remorse. There will be confession and restoration. The look of love from the Master will be the thread of faith that will pull Peter back to Jesus's side. Could this be Peter's Gethsemane?

In the upper chambers, hate is raging through the hearts of Caiaphas and the priests and scribes. They have been successful in capturing Jesus in a place away from the people, therefore avoiding conflict. He is theirs—their arrested prisoner—and mercy and compassion have gone missing. The built-up frustrations of lost theological battles, all plotted to trap Jesus, are boiling out. Anger and animosity dominate their emotions, and the decision to kill Him, while often present on their minds much earlier, was sealed when Jesus cleansed the Temple a few days ago. Now, all that remains is the legal justification for murder.

A parade of witnesses, assembled by the council, begin their "testimony" against Jesus. For more than an hour, they tell their stories and level their accusations against Jesus with no agreement, cohesion, or continuity. Truth is absent, and the council knows it. Mark's gospel tells the story: *Now the chief priests and all the council sought testimony against Jesus to put Him to death, but found none. For many bore false witness against Him, but their testimonies did not agree* (Mark 14:55-56).

Caiaphas is not concerned with truth—only that two or more witnesses testify to something worthy of sentencing Jesus to death. Therefore, the witnesses continue. Jesus is standing in their midst, praying but saying nothing. He doesn't defend Himself—He doesn't sigh in frustration.

Matthew tells us more: *But at last two false witnesses came forward and said, "This fellow said, 'I am able to destroy the temple of God and to build it in three days.'"* (Matthew 26:60b-61). Mark adds, *But not even then did their testimony agree* (Mark 14:59).

Caiaphas tries to get Jesus to incriminate Himself by asking Him to respond to the accusations—a violation of Jewish law—but Jesus remains silent. All the while, the Sanhedrin, guards, and workers are fighting their own emotions. Some begin to absorb the anger from the priests, looking at Jesus with contempt. Others simply don't know what to think or say. So, they too remain silent.

The High Priest then says to Jesus, *I put You under oath by the living God: Tell us if You are the Christ, the Son of God?* (Matthew 26:63). Jesus responds in truth, *It is as you said* (Matthew 26:64a).

Caiaphas has the evidence he wants—blasphemy! It is punishable by death to claim to be God or deity. Caiaphas tears his clothes, and gasps are heard throughout the second-floor chamber. Down below, all eyes are focused above, straining to hear what is going on. The courtyard that had suddenly become quiet is now filled with emotion, and Jesus is soon to receive its fury.

Jesus, however, is not guilty of blasphemy, for He <u>is</u> God and *He cannot deny Himself* (2 Timothy 2:13b). Caiaphas doesn't care. He is going to make everything official, even though this has been anything but an official Jewish trial. The High Priest simply says to the Sanhedrin, *You have heard His blasphemy! What do you think?* (Matthew 26:66). The response is a resounding *He is deserving death* (Matthew 26:66).Jesus's trial by ecclesiastical law is complete.

The redemptive price of sin intensifies as Jesus is mercilessly beaten, spat upon in rage, mocked, and struck repeatedly with the open hand. Blindfolded, He bears the pain—all the while praying to the Father for strength. The leaders have done a good job stirring the people against Jesus. Their pleasure with themselves only serves to embolden their assault on Jesus. But everyone present sees no anger or animosity in Jesus. There is no recoil of revenge. There is no look of disdain. There is not even a look of surprise.

Claiming an ecclesiastical victory is not enough. Caiaphas still has a problem. Roman law does not allow the Jews to execute anyone. Annas learned such years ago when the Romans removed him as High Priest.

Jesus must be tried in a Roman civil court and found guilty of a crime worthy of death. *When morning came, all the chief priests and elders of the people plotted against Jesus to put Him to death. And when they had bound Him, they led Him away and delivered Him to Pontius Pilate the governor* (Matthew 27:1-2).

Rarely does a visit from the Jewish leaders bring pleasure into the life of Pontius Pilate. Their constant pushing against the edges of Roman law for their own purposes is annoying at best. Most of the time though, their manipulative requests are frustrating—bordering on crossing the line. Though his authority allows him to take whatever drastic measures he desires, Pilate must keep the tenacious Jews in check, while still maintaining peace within Judea—Caesar demands it. Therefore, he usually placates the Jewish leaders in some fashion.

Having been forewarned that the priests were on their way, Pilate frowns as he anticipates their arrival. He has heard they are bringing their chief rival, Jesus, and they are ready to prove Him guilty of treason against Caesar. Pilate doubts this is so.

The sound of pounding feet on the street reaches the window where Pilate sits looking out over Jerusalem. Not yet in sight, the sound nonetheless has surprised Pilate. Well, not the sound itself, but rather the size of the sound. This is not the normal group of priests, scribes, and their entourage. This is much larger, and it sends a shiver through Pilate's body. Already, he does not like this.

He watches as the gathering sound turns the corner and a large body of Jewish leaders burst into view. At the front, marching with self-appointed authority and aggression, is the troublesome Chief Priest, Caiaphas. At his side appears to be the entirety of the Sanhedrin, followed by an abnormal array of bodyguards and security personnel. Tucked in the middle of all of this security is the frail and beaten frame of Jesus, bound and struggling to keep up with the brisk pace set by Caiaphas. Behind them is the rest of the Jewish contingency, including a multitude of followers and curious onlookers—most of which have not yet cleared the corner.

The scene in front of him catches Pilate off-guard, and he is quickly unsettled. Why are so many bodyguards needed to secure so fragile a soul? What are they afraid of? His alleged ability to perform miracles? A surprise attack from His followers? *What am I missing here?* Suddenly, Pilate realizes this morning is going to be bigger than he expected and anything but calm. He exits the Praetorium and enters the courtyard: *Pilate then went out to them and said, "What accusations do you bring against this Man?"* (John 18:29).

And they began to accuse Him, saying, "We found this fellow perverting the nation, and forbidding to pay taxes to Caesar, saying that He Himself is Christ, a King." Then Pilate asked Him, saying, "Are You the King of the Jews?" He answered him and said, "It is as you say" (Luke 23:2-3).

Pilate immediately recognizes another weak attempt by the Jews to get what they want. *Splitting hairs again!* he thinks. Quickly, he recognizes Jesus is not defiant nor does He appear to be a rebel or a radical insurgent. This time, Pilate is not giving in to them just to keep peace in Jerusalem. There is too much troubling him, and he responds to them, *I find no fault in the Man* (Luke 23:4b). *But they were the more fierce, saying, "He stirs up the people, teaching throughout all Judea, beginning from Galilee to this place"* (Luke 23:5).

Did they say Galilee? Is this man from Galilee? Pilate quickly verifies that it is so. He is indeed the Man from Galilee, and within minutes, Jesus is on His way to Herod, the ruler of Galilee. Pilate is using Herod to get him out of a case he has no desire to decide.

Jesus is not alone on His journey the short distance down the street to Herod's palace. The Jewish leaders and guards are again leading the way, along with the Roman soldiers sent by Pilate—and then, of course, the multitudes. For the rest of this day, there will always be the multitudes around Jesus.

Herod Antipas is the son of Herod the Great and rules Galilee and Perea as a petty local ruler. However, though limited in size and power, the rule of the Herod family is not meaningless or docile. The bloody rule of his father has filtered down to Herod Antipas, and the beheading of John the Baptist is on his resume of dastardly acts. His father is the one who wanted to kill the baby Jesus, and some of the Pharisees claim Herod Antipas wants to kill Him as well (Luke 13:31).

Herod is in Jerusalem for the Passover—not because He is Jewish—but because he wants to be where all of the action is. Pilate has sent Jesus to Herod to be tried, but he has no interest in justice. Herod is looking for a performance.

Herod is glad—Luke says, *exceedingly glad*—to see Jesus. Being from Tiberias, he has heard much about Jesus and, for a long time, has longed to see Him. Today, he is hoping to see Jesus perform one of His miracles. But Herod will not be entertained by Jesus on this day.

While the anticipation mounts within the gathering crowd, Herod proudly stands before Jesus and begins to question Him. Jesus is silent. The chief priests and scribes are vehemently hurling false accusations about Him. Yet Jesus says nothing. Prophecy is being fulfilled: *He was oppressed and He was afflicted, Yet He opened not His mouth; He was led as a lamb to the slaughter, And as a sheep before its shearers is silent, So He opened not His mouth* (Isaiah 53:7).

Dr. Ralph F. Wilson says, **"Why does Jesus remain silent amidst Herod's questions and his enemies' slanderous accusations? Jesus has always been willing to answer an honest question, but ignores empty assertions. Herod is a mere trifler—the only person to whom Jesus has nothing to say."**

The chief priests and scribes continue shouting their accusations, and then slowly, yet like a building storm, others begin to join in. Each salvo of shouts of blame becomes louder. Many, who know nothing of Jesus, join in, apparently just to feel a part of something.

Herod has had enough. With his men of war surrounding him, Herod begins to make fun of Jesus, mocking Him, ridiculing Him, and treating Him with contempt. They dress Him in an elegant robe, mocking his claim to kingship. They parade Him in front of the people, and suddenly, the angry shouts of accusation become cheers and clapping at the scene in front of them. The crowd joins the mocking and the ridiculing—their voices becoming so loud the sound of Herod and his soldiers can no longer be heard. The chief priests would normally remain smug and quiet. But even they have joined in with cheers and clapping and shouts of abuse.

Without a comment or recommendation, Herod returns Jesus to Pontius Pilate.

The scene around the Praetorium is growing ever more intense. The multitudes have grown with the return of those from Herod. The chief priests, scribes, and Pharisees have been actively stirring the crowd with false accusations against Jesus. The air is filled with emotions. Pilate is not yet rid of his worst dream.

He tries repeatedly to reason with the Jews, but they and the crowd have become demanding. There is no trial. There are no witnesses. There only remains the demand for death. Even Pilate's offer to chastise Jesus and then release Him is met with shouts of "Crucify Him!"

Then Pilate's day gets worse: *While he was sitting on the judgment seat, his wife sent to him, saying, "Have nothing to do with that just Man, for I have suffered many things today in a dream because of Him"* (Matthew 27:19).

Pontius Pilate has the power to do what is right. There is no viable evidence to kill Jesus. Three times he tells the Jews just that. While he has the power, Pilate does not have the courage to do what is right. Matthew tells the rest of the story: *When Pilate saw that he could not prevail at all, but rather that a tumult was rising, he took water and washed his hands before the multitude, saying, "I am innocent of the blood of this just Person. You see to it." And all the people answered and said, "His blood be on us and on our children"* (Matthew 27:24).

So Pilate gave sentence that it should be as they requested (Luke 23:24).

The sun has risen, and the suffering of Jesus is about to intensify. The sentence of death by crucifixion has been rendered, and Pilate, while again claiming no responsibility and again claiming he finds no fault with Jesus, has delivered Jesus to be crucified.

The scene turns painfully gory as Jesus is taken by the soldiers into the Praetorium to be scourged. Scourging is a common practice before crucifixion, designed to severely weaken a prisoner—thus bringing on a quicker death. The scourging occasionally is so severe, death itself occurs. Leather whips with bone, rock, or metal inserted in the ends will rip the flesh off the back or wherever it makes contact.

But scourging is not the only suffering Jesus is enduring. A crown of thorns is being twisted on His head, and Jesus is placed in a scarlet robe with a reed in His hand. The whole garrison of soldiers is mocking Him, spitting in His face, slapping Him with their hands, and spitefully yelling, "Hail, King of the Jews!" The reed is used to strike Him on the head. Blood streams down the face of Jesus.

In the distance, the crowds can still be heard. With each gasp of pain, a cheer rises. There is no sentiment of remorse or thought of regret. The chief priests have seen to that. Jesus is suffering. The redemptive price of sin is beyond comprehension. Yet, right now, love fills the heart and mind of Jesus.

The soldiers finally finish scourging Jesus. He has suffered more than most, but the soldiers pay no attention, nor do they care. They put His own clothes back on Him, and the road to Calvary is just ahead.

Telling the story of the suffering of Jesus is, at best, an effort in futility. Words become hollow and inadequate. Even the most accomplished of writers grapple with extracting from the language deserving words. The video industry improves the effort as it is added to the written word. But even then, there is left a large gap that remains untold. Nonetheless, it is a story that is often told. Indeed, it is a story that must be told.

The road to Golgotha or Calvary is not long—unless you have been beaten and scourged and tormented for several hours. For Jesus, the cross on which He will be crucified is a weight that brings Him to His knees. The physical abuse is having its intended effect. While excruciating to watch, the Father is not intervening for His Son. Even Jesus, who has the power to stop this cruel and evil attack, does not do so. The Messiah moves willingly toward His sacrifice of death.

The cross is placed on the back of Jesus, and His knees give a little before He is able to straighten them again and stabilize His balance. Jesus is dreadfully weary and weak.

He begins to take His first steps on the Via Dolorosa, "The Sorrowful Way." The path's narrow way makes the volume of people lining its sides seem much more than what is really there. However, the crowds are by no means small. With barely room to pass by, the steps of Jesus are slow and agonizing. The soldiers are impatient with the pace. They push and prod Jesus along. But helping Him along they are not!

The crowds look on. The soldiers march on. The high priests and scribes are tagging on, and Jesus is struggling along—stumbling under the weight of a heavy cross. Jeers are still present, and shouts of ridicule are still coming from those being spurred on by the scribes and Pharisees. But nowhere are there shouts of "Hosanna! Hosanna! Hosanna in the highest!" The triumphal entry is but a distant and foggy memory.

Scripture tells us very little about the journey to Golgotha. We know Simon the Cyrenian was chosen to carry His cross. We know Jesus spoke to the women who were lamenting for Him saying, *Daughters of Jerusalem, do not weep for Me, but weep for yourselves and for your children* (Luke 23:28b). We know there was *a great multitude of people following Him* (verse 27). But we know little else.

Therefore, let us paint our own picture while diligently attempting to be true to what it might have actually been like. Who is here along the Via Dolorosa, and who are these people that comprise the multitudes?

The chief priests, scribes, Pharisees, and all the other religious leaders are here—be sure of that. They have planned and orchestrated this whole event, and they are seeing it through to the end. They are pleased with themselves—proud with their plan to dispose of the problematic Jesus. But deep within their soul, there is an unsettled spirit—not strong enough to cause them to change their course of action but there nonetheless. For the more sympathetic among the Sanhedrin, that unsettled spirit is a gnawing in their gut that will not go away.

Who are the people in the multitudes? Where are they from, and how many of them have seen Jesus in a different setting at a different place? Passover draws faithful Jews to Jerusalem from as far away as they can travel. Some estimates say millions are here this year. So, let's make some safe assumptions.

Standing and watching are some of the five thousand who tasted of the fish and loaves on that hillside of Galilee. They heard the Teacher speak about the kingdom of God, and they saw Him heal those in need of healing. What are their thoughts at this moment? Have their thoughts of Jesus been so contaminated by the chief priests that they too have been shouting, "Crucify Him?!" Or has the teaching of Jesus so impacted them that they are compassionate toward Him—maybe confused and silent, but compassionate—as the vivid memories of that hillside in Galilee tell them of a different man? Does Jesus recognize them, and do His eyes reassure them to not be afraid?

Some among this multitude, along the Via Dolorosa, heard Jesus say, *Blessed are the poor in spirit, for theirs is the kingdom of heaven,* (Matthew 5:3) as they sat on the mountainside overlooking the Sea of

Galilee. Did Jesus see them then, and does He see them now? What are their thoughts? Is the look from Jesus so soft and understanding that their minds go back to Galilee and His teaching? Does Jesus glance over the people, looking at them one by one, praying for their doubts and their fragile faith? Or is the pain so great that Jesus is only focusing on the next step?

The thieves and the pickpockets are here for certain. With all the attention given to Jesus and the procession that is slowly moving along the path of the Via Dolorosa, business has been very good and, honestly, quite easy. Jesus knows they are here, and the weight of their sin is added to the load of sin Jesus carries for the world. Jesus prays for the thieves as, one by one, He spots them in the crowd. Do their eyes meet His, and do they hurry away knowing Jesus knows all about them?

How many in the crowd are followers of Jesus—undocumented by scripture? The impact and scope of Jesus's ministry has been huge. More than once, scripture tells us of the many who believed on that day. But what about the pain and emotion these followers are experiencing just now? Those who are weak in faith—what are the thoughts and emotions within them?

And where are the eleven?

The inscription on the cross, "THE KING OF THE JEWS," seemingly glistens as it is raised into place with Jesus hanging in pain upon it. The nails used to secure the body draw their own measure of blood from His body. On each side are robbers suffering their own pain. But their burden bears only the weight of their own sin. For Jesus, the redemptive price of the sin of the world and the coming separation from the Father is a burden that outstrips comprehension. The Messiah's time has come.

It is only 9:00 a.m., and so much has transpired since Jesus rose from His knees in Gethsemane and allowed the kiss of betrayal and His arrest. His apostles are gone, and the journey has indeed been a "Lonely Road, Up Calvary's Way." The pain and agony of the past six hours have brought Jesus near death—yet death is still six hours away.

It seems as though all of Jerusalem and her guests have converged at the hill of Golgotha—that hill called Calvary. The air is filled with emotions—some strong feelings of violence, some angry, some confused, and some sad. For those who have come to know Jesus, there are tears. And hate looms large in the hearts of many.

Mark tells us:

> *And those who passed by blasphemed Him, wagging their heads and saying, "Aha! You who destroy the temple and build it in three days, save Yourself, and come down from the cross!" Likewise the chief priests also, mocking among themselves with the scribes, said, "He saved others; Himself He cannot save. Let the Christ, the King of Israel, descend now from the cross, that we may see and believe." Even those who were crucified with Him reviled Him.*
>
> – Mark 15:29-32

The words of Psalm 22:7a are coming to life: *All those who see Me ridicule Me.*

While the chief priests and scribes continue to stir up the people, the Roman soldiers need no prodding. Their abuse during His scourging at the Praetorium continues as Jesus hangs on the cross. They are indifferent to the suffering on full display in front of them. As they divide Christ's garments and cast lots for them and ridicule Him as "King of the Jews," the crowd waits for Jesus to die—some with hearts that are glad—others with deep sorrow. Three hours pass by. We are not told, but eternity will reveal how many people's eyes will look into the eyes of Jesus this day. What are they seeing, and do they feel the love of an eternal God as His eyes meet theirs?

As noon (sixth hour) settles in, all of the land sinks into darkness. The suffering of Jesus intensifies. There have now been three hours of excruciating physical pain. There have been three hours of the body losing its battle to death. The picture of Christ suffering on the cross numbs the senses. But for Jesus, death is still three hours away.

As the physical suffering continues, the Messiah is contending with the brutal forces of evil as well. Are we to think that the powers of this world would allow the redemptive price of sin to be paid without a battle — an epic battle? Oh no! This day is the ultimate of all spiritual battles. It is the moment when Satan unleashes all of his fury to stop God's master plan to rescue mankind. Just now, the agony of Jesus becomes the battle to conquer evil; and darkness becomes a force on the streets of Jerusalem — at the hill called Calvary. This day is everything.

If Jesus is really the Messiah, He must not only overcome Satan, but He must also absorb the wrath of God.

> **During the three hours which the darkness continued, Jesus was in agony, wrestling with the powers of darkness, and <u>suffering His Father's displeasure against the sin of man</u>, for which He was now making His soul an offering. Never were there three such hours since the day God created man upon the earth, never such a dark and awful scene; it was the turning point of that great affair, man's redemption and salvation.**
>
> – Matthew Henry

Despite the presence of evil, the struggle of these three hours of darkness is not really a battle at all. It is a willing Messiah, reaching into His vault of love, offering redemption to a fallen world. Yes, evil is raging its fury; yes, Satan is unleashing his full array of demons. But the suffering of Jesus is not from overcoming Satan. The suffering of Jesus is in redeeming my sin and your sin and the world's sin.

And she will bring forth a Son, and you shall call His name JESUS, for <u>He will save His people from their sins</u> (Matthew 1:21).

He will save His people from their sins. Let us pause and reflect on what that statement means. Sin has a price: *For the wages of sin is death* .

. . (Romans 6:23a). The penalty for each and every sin I commit demands death, and I would be gravely mistaken to marginalize that thought.

God hates sin, and it is on sin that He will pour out His wrath. All of the fury, all of the anger, all of the power, all of the punishment that God has withheld is reserved for sin. Make no mistake, there is a dreadful and horrible price for sin.

Right now, as He suffers on the cross, Jesus is paying that price. Jesus is redeeming you from your sin. Jesus is the propitiation for your sin. Jesus is stepping in front of the wrath that you have earned—taking the bullet for you. It is the sacrificial blood of Jesus that is being poured out for our sin. The spiritual punishment being received by Jesus is indescribable. Jesus is dying for you and me. Jesus is bearing the wrath of the Father, and the Father is not holding back. We focus so much on the pain of a cruel cross—the nails in His hands and the side that was pierced—but it is the agony of sin that has caused Jesus to be forsaken by the Father. *For God so loved the world that He gave His only begotten Son, that whoever believes in Him should not perish but have everlasting life* (John 3:16).

My sin is covered by the blood of Jesus. Your sin is covered by the blood of Jesus. The blood that He is shedding, as He hangs here, is filled with the power of a loving God that is giving a condemned world spiritual freedom. I wonder which drop that trickles down His cheek is blotting out my sin—and how large of a drop is required?

Around the crosses on the hill of Golgotha, the people wander and pause and ponder. The jeering has mostly stopped. The darkness has silenced even the morbid joy of Jesus's adversaries. The scene is just too somber. Much of the crowd has left, unable to stomach the tragic picture of reality playing out on the "Place of the Skull."

It is now the ninth hour (3:00 p.m.). There is an eerie silence on Golgotha. The darkness has dispersed the crowds. Those still lingering are filled with uncertainty and even fear. Striving to sort out what is happening is producing no answers—not even unlikely ones. Their minds flash back over the recent hours—replaying moment after moment. Never have they seen anything like this. Even those who regularly attend crucifixions admit such.

Jesus has fulfilled His mission as the Messiah:

- *After this, Jesus, knowing that <u>all things were now accomplished</u>, that the Scripture might be fulfilled, said, "I thirst!" Now a vessel full of sour wine was sitting there; and they filled a sponge with sour wine, put it on hyssop, and put it to His mouth. So when Jesus had received the sour wine, He said, **"It is finished!"** And bowing His head, He gave up His spirit* (John 19:28-30).
- *And at the ninth hour Jesus cried out with a loud voice, saying, "Eloi, Eloi, lama sabachthani?" which is translated,* **"My God, My God, why have You forsaken Me?"** (Mark 15:34).
- *And when Jesus had cried out with a loud voice, He said,* **"Father, into Your hands I commit My spirit."** *Having said this, He breathed His last* (Luke 23:46).

It is finished. Those nearby watch Jesus breathe His last. Those expecting Jesus to perform a miracle and climb down from the cross feel deflated. The high priests and scribes whisper, "It is finally over!" The women and other followers of Jesus are too grieved to even think—their minds and emotions frozen in time. They simply look up at the body of Jesus hanging limp on the cross, and they weep.

But suddenly, during this time of arrested emotions, all of nature cries out. The apostles are gone. The disciples are gone. The crowds have dispersed. But nature is paying attention. A few days ago, during the triumphal entry, the Pharisees asked Jesus to quiet His disciples: *Teacher, rebuke Your disciples*. But Jesus said to them, *I tell you that if these should keep silent, the stones would immediately cry out* (Luke 19:40b).

It is now nature's turn, and nature will not be silenced. He who created all things is not being abandoned by His creation. Scripture does not record it, yet surely, all of nature is speaking. Man may not understand the language spoken. History may not acclaim its significance. Yet we have already been taught nature's love for its Creator:

- *And every creature which is in heaven and on the earth and under the earth and such as are in the sea, and all that are in them, I*

heard saying: *"Blessing and honor and glory and power be to Him who sits on the throne, and to the Lamb, forever and ever!"* (Revelation 5:13).
- *The mountains and the hills shall break forth into singing before you, and all the trees of the field shall clap their hands* (Isaiah 55:12b).
- *All the earth shall worship You and sing praises to You; they shall sing praises to Your name* (Psalm 66:4).

Listen for just a minute: The trees are speaking as the wind filters through their leaves—their sound a rustling tone of praise. On the distant peak, the little sparrow is warbling its constant tune of love—remembering the One who feeds it. The squirrel leaps from branch to branch, pausing frequently to view the Messiah below, shouting out its frequent chirps of awe.

The owl, somewhat confused by the darkness, has come out of its burrow and is joining in nature's symphony—hooting its hymn of thanks that somewhat resembles the sound of a tuba. Even the burro, attached to the hitch nearby, brays an occasional haunting cry to his Maker hanging on the hill nearby. And now, as we listen closely, surely, we can hear all of creation crying out to Jesus—each in its own language—each with its own passion—each lifting their special voice to the King of Kings and the Lord of Lords—and to the Messiah, who hangs on the cross.

Scripture, however, does indeed record nature speaking out at the very moment that Jesus dies—and that in not so gentle a voice. The massive veil of the Temple is splitting in two from top to bottom. The veil is approximately sixty feet wide, thirty feet tall, and four inches thick and takes 300 priests to move it, and yet it lies silent on the floor—split from top to bottom—not by the hands of man or the violence of a quake, but by God Himself.

But why did God split the veil? The veil separates the Holy of Holies, where God resides, from the presence of sinful man. Since Jesus has just paid the price for our sin, there is no longer a need for the veil. Man can now come to God directly through his repentance. The price has just been paid in full!

The earth is now quaking, and fear grips the heart of every person. The rumbling is producing a panic all around. The earth is shouting to its

Maker, but people everywhere are running about in fear and screams of horror ring out into the darkness, somewhat drowning out nature's choir.

The earth is not out of harmony with itself. This is not a seismic adjustment of tectonic plates deep within the earth. This is creation understanding the magnitude of the last six hours. The Messiah has come. The Messiah has fulfilled the command of the Father, and as Jesus cries, "It is finished," all of nature is to be heard!

The rocks are indeed crying out. Their journey from the cliffs above is a bumpy, yet not silent, fall to the ground below. As they land and shatter with a voice unavoidable, people are scattering and running for their lives. Nature is indeed being heard. The disciples are still elsewhere.

In the midst of nature's roars and its shout of "Hosanna! Hosanna! Hosanna in the Highest!" there is a miracle occurring. Matthew tells the story: *So when the centurion and those with him, who were guarding Jesus, saw the earthquake and the things that had happened, they feared greatly, saying,* ***"Truly this was the Son of God!"*** (Matthew 27:54).

With those words, the very ones who placed Jesus on the cross and ridiculed Him and beat Him are acknowledging He is indeed the Son of God! The Centurion cries out, as nature shouts out its praise to the Messiah, words of belief: ***Truly this was the Son of God!***

Believe on the Lord Jesus Christ, and you will be saved, you and your household (Acts 16:31b).

Therefore, because it was the Preparation Day, that the bodies should not remain on the cross on the Sabbath (for that Sabbath was a high day), the Jews asked Pilate that their legs might be broken, and that they might be taken away. Then the soldiers came and broke the legs of the first and of the other who was crucified with Him. But when they came to Jesus and saw that He was already dead, they did not break His legs. But one of the soldiers pierced His side with a spear, and immediately blood and water came out. And he who has seen has testified,

> *and his testimony is true; and he knows that he is telling the truth, so that you may believe. For these things were done that the Scripture should be fulfilled, "Not one of His bones shall be broken." And again another Scripture says, "They shall look on Him whom they pierced."*
>
> – John 19:31-37

The soldiers and the curious have left. The darkness has vanished, and the city of Jerusalem is confused and battered. The once unnoticed hill of Golgotha will henceforth be a notorious landmark—revered by millions and the object of countless writings and songs.

Pilate has released the body of Jesus to Joseph of Arimathea. He takes it to a new tomb he has recently hewn out of rock. Mary Magdalene and Mary the mother of James sit nearby and watch as Joseph and his friend Nicodemus prepare the body for burial.

> *And Nicodemus, who at first came to Jesus by night, also came, bringing a mixture of myrrh and aloes, about a hundred pounds. Then they took the body of Jesus, and bound it in strips of linen with the spices, as the custom of the Jews is to bury. Now in the place where He was crucified there was a garden, and in the garden a new tomb in which no one had yet been laid. So there they laid Jesus, because of the Jews' Preparation Day, for the tomb was nearby.*
>
> – John 19:39-42

It is late in the day on the Day of Preparation. The Jews are finishing their tasks—each tediously keeping the law's instructions. Jesus's body lies in the tomb. The tension of the day has eased, yet an unsettled spirit has enveloped Jerusalem. The day of the Messiah is closing with the falling sunset.

But the amazing story of Jesus, the Christ, is not yet finished.

LIFE APPLICATION

And Jesus cried out with a loud voice, and breathed His last (Mark 1:37).

The disciples walked away from Jesus, just like He said they would. Our first reaction is one of disbelief and condemnation. How could the very men Jesus chose—the selected twelve—run from the presence of their Master? How could they leave Jesus after all of the miracles and truths He had shown them and taught them? How could all of them be so weak and cowardly?

However, before we look on the disciples with accusing hearts and thoughts, let us ask ourselves these questions:

Question: When have I walked away from Jesus? When have I decided to do things on my own and in my own way? When did I last choose a path I knew was wrong or selfish? And what am I going to change in my life so that I won't be abandoning Jesus?

Sin separates us from God. God and sin cannot co-exist. It is an eternal separation from our Creator that will leave the unbeliever forever separated from the power and the love of God.

Jesus, in the dying moments of His life, as the full load of our sin met the full measure of the Father's wrath, felt the impact of being separated from the Father. Never before had Jesus, the man, not felt the presence of the Father. When being tempted by Satan—the Father was there. When facing the precipice in Bethlehem—the Father was there. But on the cross, with our sin on His shoulders, the Father abandoned the Son. And Jesus cried out, "My God, My God, why have You forsaken Me?"

Question: What sin in your life is causing you to feel the lack of God's presence? What are you going to do about it? What changes in your life, your service, your heart, and your mind are you going to make to assure you feel God's presence?

Chapter Ten

> "The clock ticks slowly on Holy Saturday, pressing reactionaries beyond their capacities. It is a day fashioned for handwringing."
>
> Anonymous

For you will not leave my soul among the dead or allow your Holy One to rot in the grave (Acts 2:27, NLT)

Passion Week – Day Seven
Sabbath Saturday

On the day that tragedy comes into your life, everything becomes enshrouded in a mental fog. The events, as they unfold throughout the day, are dimmed to the mind. Everything feels like a dream—as though blurred by the darkness of night. Thoughts are clouded by emotions, and grief overwhelms the mind. You do what you need to do—not really knowing what you are doing, how you are doing it, or if you are doing it properly. But somehow, you get through the day—often aided by the release of tears of sorrow. That day of tragedy was yesterday.

However, the next day often seems worse. The shock is subsiding and the pain of reality has passed its initial stage. Now, the mind begins to race in a thousand different directions at once. Shock is slowly being replaced by deep sorrow, and the questions of "Why?" are never really answered.

Today is that next day in Jerusalem. It is the day following the day of the murder of the Teacher—the Christ—the Messiah—the One who has healed and impacted so many lives. It is the day following the day when darkness appeared at noon and the earth shook and rocks fell from the hillside. Today is a day of immense confusion, and the people in Jerusalem this day are engulfed in a Sabbath Saturday they were not expecting. This is the next day, and the body of Jesus remains sealed in the tomb.

As we attempt to sort out the events of today, scripture provides few details. We will ever be cognizant of that fact. However, there is still much that can be said and reasonably gleaned from what this day contains for a whole array of people. Let us endeavor to do so.

> What happened on Saturday between Good Friday and Easter? To the untrained eye, nothing at all! If we were to go to the tomb outside of Jerusalem at the crack of dawn on Saturday we would observe little of major significance. The body of a recently crucified man would be on a slab in a tomb—bloodied, discolored, rigid with rigor mortis. It would be a hideous sight (if we could see it). But we can't because it is behind a sealed boulder that plugs the entrance.
>
> But in heaven above and on earth beneath, far from our human senses, there is enough activity to change eternity. Demons are raging; some shrieking in fear. Satan has been stripped of all authority and power. Christ has opened paradise, ushering in both the thief who died by Him on the cross, and all those who had believed in the Coming Messiah through the ages. The angels of heaven are rejoicing. The dead man's Father no longer has His back turned toward His Son. There is a sense that a celebration is about to erupt at any moment! That is why Saturday is so important on the church calendar.

Yet back in Jerusalem, on the surface of Planet Earth, it is business as usual.

– Taken from the sermon "It is Saturday, But Is It Finished?" by Pastor Roger Steven Warner (March 11, 2013)

Let us remind ourselves that all too often, we permit ourselves to be prisoners of the natural realm. What we can see, what we can hear, what we can feel, and the world in which we physically exist captivates our thoughts and is the dominating force in our lives.

That is exactly what the day of Sabbath Saturday was like to just about everyone in Jerusalem—including the disciples. Jesus is dead, and now what do we do? How do we pick up the pieces and try to move on? Locked doors and feeble efforts to comfort each other was as far as the followers of Jesus could move forward.

But in the spiritual realm, Jesus was not locked up in a beaten and bruised body. Jesus was opening up Paradise and leading the captive and ascending on high and descending into the lower parts of the earth. And He was doing such that *He might fulfill all things* (Ephesians 4:10b).

To further understand what was happening in the spiritual realm on Sabbath Saturday, read Acts 2:23-31 and Ephesians 4:8-10 and 1 Peter 3:19-20.

Sleep eluded many in Jerusalem last night—particularly those whose names will forever be linked to the story of the crucifixion of Jesus. The images and the rawness of yesterday haunt the mind, and the intensity of this crucifixion leaves an unsettled feeling deep in their gut.

Those who were observers of the events of yesterday are filled with questions: *What was this all about? Who was this Jesus, and did He really have supernatural powers? If so, why didn't He use them?* The questions that circulate through their minds are countless. The answers to those questions are absent.

If anyone had a sleepless night last night, it was Caiaphas, the Sanhedrin, and all the scribes and Pharisees. Jesus is dead, just as they had desired, and yet they still fear Him. They are worried about Jesus, they are worried about His disciples, and they are worried about the people. Matthew tells the story:

> *On the next day, which followed the Day of Preparation, the chief priests and Pharisees gathered together to Pilate, saying, "Sir, we remember, while He was still alive, how that deceiver said, 'After three days I will rise.' Therefore command that the tomb be made secure until the third day, lest His disciples come by night and steal Him away, and say to the people, 'He has risen from the dead.' So the last deception will be worse than the first.'" Pilate said to them, "You have a guard; go your way, make it as secure as you know how." So they went and made the tomb secure, sealing the stone and setting the guard.*
>
> – Matthew 27:62-66

Pontius Pilate is trying to clear yesterday out of his mind—with little or no success. He indeed is one of those who is facing today with severe sleep deprivation. The words of warnings from his wife repeat themselves endlessly in his mind, and the feeling in his gut tells him it all went so wrong yesterday. Oh, it is not that he has any concern or regard for this man Jesus—He probably deserved death for something. It is just a feeling that something greater is at work here and he doesn't know what it is. He sits looking out over the courtyard of his palace, and the images of yesterday's events, which played out in this very courtyard, are so real they almost seem to be happening again. Pilate shifts uncomfortably in his chair.

Without warning, the familiar chatter of the Jewish chief priests and Pharisees bring a warning to Pilate, and immediately, the group makes its appearance around the corner. Pilate is not ready for this—not on this Saturday morning. He braces himself, hopes deep within himself that they will turn and go away, and determines he will not yield to their demands. With that, he goes to meet them.

After hearing their story, Pilate reasons within himself: "The man is dead, my soldiers have pierced His side to make sure, and I have released His body to the wealthy Joseph of Arimathea, a man of impeccable reputation. Could it be they are worried about His claim that He will arise from the dead?"

Pilate listens to their story but is unmoved. Their request for Roman guards to protect the tomb is emphatically denied with the words *You have a guard; go your way, make it as secure as you know how.* Pilate wants nothing else to do with Jesus or the Jews—not on this day!

The scribes and Pharisees and chief priests ponder their options and quickly realize there are none. So, they do, indeed, proceed to the tomb, first securing it and sealing it—then placing their own guards in front of it. Their task is complete, but they feel no better about the situation. Somehow, they know there is more to come.

I will strike the Shepherd and the sheep of the flock will be scattered (Matthew 26:31b).

The sheep are indeed scattered! Jesus had told them they would leave Him in fear. They all denied it. Peter brashly vocalized it: *If I have to die with You, I will not deny You! And all the others said likewise* (Mark 14:31b). But scattered they are. Judas is dead, and the other eleven have fled—the scriptures tell us not where.

Fear is a powerful emotion, and escape is its outlet. It is, at least in part, instinctual, particularly when survival is at stake. For the disciples, the experience in the Garden of Gethsemane caused them to flee. They were terrified.

But where did they go? We do not fully know. We do know Peter and John were nearby when Jesus was tried before Pilate and maybe Herod. We do know others may have been hiding amongst the crowds at His crucifixion. However, there is no direct mention of any of them saying or doing anything. Where are they today—this dreadful day after the day their Lord was crucified? There has been much speculation: they returned to Galilee, they returned to Bethany, they gathered in the Upper Room, or they just remained in Jerusalem. All we know is the sheep are scattered, and scripture leaves it at that. However, let us paint some reasonable pictures.

Let's start with Peter. Peter is not with the others. But why? Peter is one of the leaders of the group. Peter, with James and John, was the first level of disciples that Jesus often turned to for special moments or tasks. Though he doesn't know it now, Peter has been chosen by Jesus, along with John, to lead the disciples into spreading the gospel. Peter is a leader—but not today. Peter is alone. But why?

It is probably because Peter has a lot of soul searching to do and the guilt and shame of his denial of Jesus is ripping at his heart. Peter is hurting within. He is in a mental and spiritual state of collapse. Peter can still hear the rooster crowing. And now, Jesus is dead. It is almost more than Peter can handle. The teachings of Jesus about His death and resurrection are not reaching Peter's conscious mind—the pain is just too great.

However, that brief look from Jesus, from the upper level at Caiaphas's palace, is still fresh in Peter's mind, serving as a lifeline that Peter is now desperately clinging to. Peter will recover. But right now, he needs to be alone.

It is likely that some or all of the other apostles are staying close together. Their fear is not gone—maybe diminished a little—but not gone. What conversation is happening and what thoughts are rushing through their minds is only speculation. However, let us speculate cautiously.

Mostly they are waiting—not sure what to do or where to go. They lean on each other for strength—each drawing from the friendships cultivated over the past three years. They talk about the strength and presence of Jesus and His wisdom so deep that answers to questions always seemed to bring thoughts of *Why didn't I think of that?*

The conversation has surely arisen concerning the three times Jesus talked about His suffering and death at the hands of the priests and scribes and His declaration that He would be raised from the dead. Could it actually be so?

They recall the first time in Caesarea Philippi, when Peter exclaimed it would not be so and Jesus rebuked him. And then the second time while in Galilee, when He said, *The Son of Man is about to be betrayed into the hands of men, and they will kill Him, and the third day He will be raised up* (Matthew 17:22-23). And they recall how exceedingly sorrowful they were as they gazed into the eyes of the Master. And then just a short time ago, while heading to Jerusalem, He took them to the side of the road and told them He would be betrayed, mocked, scourged, and crucified, and on the third day, He would arise again. If this is indeed so, they must wait. Maybe their faith is weak—maybe they are confused. Certainly, they are afraid. But together, they wait for Jesus.

They spend the time in conversation and prayer—discussing yesterday, the last few days, and Jesus. Mostly, they are talking about Jesus. The disciples talk openly, drawing strength from each other, praying together, and they wait.

Mary, the mother of Jesus, is in the area of Jerusalem—probably under the care of John. But exactly where she is, we do not know. It is difficult to think of Mary and not attach the word "grieving." Mary is in deep sorrow today. Yes, it is true she fully understands the purpose of Jesus coming to earth. Yes, she understands He is not really hers—He is only borrowed for a season. Yes, Mary knows He will arise again—the victor over sin and death.

However, the pain of yesterday is too real not to grieve. Her faith is not shaken, nor is she sorrowful for the mission of Jesus. But the images of yesterday, imbedded in her memory, do nothing to ease the pain in her heart. Why, oh why, did it have to be this way? Mary prays and asks for strength to take another breath and to make it through another day. At the moment that He whispered those words, "It is finished!" Mary lost her Son. Jesus is no longer her Son—He is now her Savior.

We could paint a picture of many others on this day. What about Mary Magdalene, Nicodemus, Joseph of Arimathea, Herod, Pontius Pilate, Pilate's wife, the families of the two thieves crucified beside Jesus? Each one is having their own day of emotions. Yesterday changed the life of all who were part of the story or an observer of the story. Take a moment to select a few from the list above or maybe one of your own—like the Roman guard. Step into their shoes: what are they feeling and thinking today?

What about the other religious leaders or those who saw Jesus in Galilee, those who were shouting, "Hosanna! Hosanna! Hosanna in the Highest!" as they walked down Palm Sunday Way. And what about the healed blind or the walking lame or the souls no longer demon possessed? What are they experiencing today? What are they thinking today? Where are they today?

There can be much speculation about the emotions of Sabbath Saturday. Pastor Gerrit Scott Dawson says:

> **Jesus was dead.** *Could this really be the end of Him? Yes, He had predicted that He would rise on the third day. But the disciples in their grief either forgot that promise or no longer believed it (or perhaps had never really understood it). The revolting sounds of Good Friday kept spilling into the eerie quiet of His absence. They waited, but with little, if any, hope. On this barren seventh day, those who loved Jesus hid behind locked doors in fear and despair.*
>
> – Taken from desiringgod.org

Look again at this last line: *On this barren seventh day, those who loved Jesus hid behind locked doors in fear and despair.*

So it is on Sabbath Saturday—the day after the Messiah was crucified.

LIFE APPLICATION

I am weary with my crying; my throat is parched; My eyes fail while I wait for my God (Psalm 69:3, NASB).

As we vividly pointed out in Chapter Two, waiting, especially waiting patiently, can be a very challenging time. The process and mindset becomes even more difficult when we must wait for the uncertain. Waiting for what you know is going to happen is one thing, but waiting for the uncertain is much more painful. Especially if fear for one's well-being is in question.

Waiting on the Lord is often difficult. However, Isaiah 40:31 tells us it is worth it:

> *But those who wait on the LORD*
> *Shall renew their strength;*
> *They shall mount up with wings like eagles,*
> *They shall run and not be weary,*
> *They shall walk and not faint.*

Question: What are you having trouble waiting on the Lord for? A decision? Provisions? Peace? Joy? What truths of God's Word are you claiming to give you peace while you wait? Search out the verses on waiting in the Bible.

Pastor Warner pointed out that while we wait impatiently in life, God is not sitting idly by. Often without your knowledge, God is moving *"for the good of them that love Him, according to His purposes* (Romans 8:28). Please remember that God has your well-being in mind.

Question: Do you trust God? Do you trust God enough to wait on Him? Do you trust God enough to wait on Him with patience and joy and peace?

Chapter Eleven

> "If Jesus rose from the dead, then you have to accept all that he said; if he didn't rise from the dead, then why worry about any of what he said? The issue on which everything hangs is not whether or not you like his teaching but whether or not he rose from the dead."
>
> Tim Keller

Do not be afraid, for I know that you seek Jesus who was crucified. He is not here; for He is risen, as He said. Come, see the place where the Lord lay. And go quickly and tell His disciples that He is risen from the dead, and indeed He is going before you into Galilee; there you will see Him. Behold, I have told you (Matthew 28:5b-7).

Passion Week – Day Eight
Resurrection Sunday

The second day after a tragedy is not much better than the first. The world still feels upside down. Emotions are no better; fears are still keeping the soul and mind in captivity. Oh, it may be a speck of change better, but not much. It is a new week—the Sabbath is over, and the limitations of the holy day are expired. People may get on with the things halted by the Sabbath.

Day eight is here. It is the last day of the eight days that changed the spiritual world forever. Without day eight, there is no purpose or meaning to the other seven days. Without day eight, the purpose of the Messiah would be incomplete. Without day eight, the fractured bond between man and God would still be fractured. Without day eight, Paul says, *And **if Christ is not risen**, then our preaching is empty and your faith is also empty* (1 Corinthians 15:14).

*And **if Christ is not risen**, your faith is futile; you are still in your sins! Then also those who have fallen asleep in Christ have perished. If in this life only we have hope in Christ, **we are of all men the most pitiable*** (1 Corinthians 15:17-19).

He is not here; for He is risen, as He said (Matthew 28:6). These words, by the angel at the tomb of Jesus, declares a truth that changes everything. With this truth, we can discard all of the "is not risen" effects about the resurrection—being the most pitiable, futile faith, empty preaching, and still being in our sins are all irrelevant. This day is everything because on this day, the miracle of miracles happened—Jesus arose from the dead and is alive!

With the truth of the successful sacrifice of the Messiah, the spiritual imbalance of the universe has been righted. Man's fractured relationship with a perfect God has been mended. The law has been fulfilled, and eternal life is available for all mankind.

It is a day of joy and jubilation! It is a day to celebrate! The Savior of the world has risen from the dead!

Dawn is fighting its way to the horizon. Brisk is the air and clear is the sky that will be revealed once the sun exposes the splendor of a new day. Most of Jerusalem still is in slumber, but Mary Magdalene and a few other women have been waiting for today. They have prepared spices to anoint the body of Jesus. Unable to do so on the Sabbath, yesterday, they waited—but with little if any patience. They are anxious to get to the tomb.

It is just before dawn as they pack their spices and head to the tomb, uncertain of what they will find. On the way, the women are mostly silent. They pull their garments tightly around their upper torsos and neck, attempting to combat the light but cold air of the early morning. Their only discussion concerns how they are going to roll the rock away from the entrance. Mark explains, *And they said among themselves, "Who will roll away the stone from the door of the tomb for us?"* (Mark 16:3).

The answer is revealed by Matthew: *Now after the Sabbath, as the first day of the week began to dawn, Mary Magdalene and the other Mary came to see the tomb. And behold, there was a great earthquake; for an angel of the Lord descended from heaven, and came and rolled back the stone from the door, and sat on it* (Matthew 28:1-2).

As the women approach the tomb, a great earthquake brings them to a halt. Fear envelops them, causing them to scream out as the earth vibrates under their feet. They stumble around—running to and away from each other. Running around is futile as the whole earth quakes. But not moving seems wrong too.

The women's minds flash back to Friday, when darkness was the companion of another quake. They recall the fear of that moment also. But along with the memory of that quake is the horror of Jesus hanging dead on the cross. The vivid picture arrests their breathing—just as it did two days ago. They choke with nausea, turning their heads away as they gag over the picture in their mind that feels so real. The pain and sorrow they feel will take forever to heal. They slowly gather themselves—one by one—until all have regained their composure. My, how painful this day is feeling!

The quaking of the earth is violent—but lasts just a few moments. To the women, it feels like an eternity. As the earth settles and the women slowly catch their breath, before them, sitting on the stone to the tomb, is an angel. Matthew says, *His countenance was like lightning and his clothes as white as snow* (Matthew 28:3). Mark says he was *clothed in a long white robe sitting on the right side; and they were alarmed* (Mark 16:5). Luke says there were two angels *in shining garments* (Luke 24:4b).

The message to the frightened women brings great fear and joy: *For I know that you seek Jesus who was crucified. He is not here; for He is risen, as He said. Come see the place where the Lord lay. And go quickly and tell His disciples that He is risen from the dead . . .* (Matthew 28:5b-7a).

The women leave: *So they went out quickly and fled from the tomb, for they trembled and were amazed. And they said nothing to anyone, for they were afraid* (Mark 16:8).

There is no purposeful reason to paint a word picture more vivid than what scripture says in Matthew 28:4. The women are at the tomb; the angel, with his countenance like lightning and clothes as white as snow, sits nearby, and Matthew pens these words: *And the guards shook for fear of him, and became like dead men.*

Whether they had been sleeping or not, the guards are now fully awake and deeply in fear. These brave soldiers, assigned by the Chief Priest to guard the tomb of Jesus—these seasoned and experienced warriors—are lying as though they are comatose on the ground. Matthew says nothing more about them—nothing else needs to be said.

The power of the forces of God have the ability to bring the strongest and the toughest to their knees. The guards shook for fear of him. This "him" is not Jesus—it is not HIM! It is not the Holy Spirit, sent down to make a couple of corrections on earth. This 'him" is not God, the Father, standing over the guards to judge them. No, the guards are in fear of an angel—a created being of the Most High. Oft times, in scripture, God unleashes His power, and man has no defense against it.

However, sometimes God uses a man or an angel to carry out His will—with all the power and authority necessary. God has sent an angel to move the stone and to instruct the women to go tell the disciples that Jesus has risen. The guards are fearful—and well they should be. They lie as dead before the empty tomb.

The women are gone, angels are no longer visible, and there is no body for the guards to keep watch over. They slowly right themselves— shamefully gathering themselves. They begin to look around for any clues that would help them in their dilemma. They gather for a moment to ponder their situation and then slowly and reluctantly head to the city to report to the chief priests what has happened. It is trip they are dreading.

If the chief priests think things are calming down—they are sadly wrong. Their ongoing fears of Jesus are valid. Their criminal acts and evil hearts are leaving a trail of guilt all the way to the house of Caiaphas and the Sanhedrin. And now, this week is starting out dreadfully.

The solution for the religious leaders always seems to be birthed in an assembly of the priests and the elders—and even the Sanhedrin. This is certainly the case this time. They meet, they confer, they consult together, and the solution is money—lots of it. Lots of money given to the guards to lie: *When they had assembled with the elders and consulted together, they gave a large sum of money to the soldiers, saying, "Tell them, 'His disciples came at night and stole Him away while we slept'"* (Matthew 28:12-13). Deceit is the smoke screen sin uses to cover its trail of guilt.

Peter and John are running. They are running to the tomb of Jesus. It is a race not to see who is fastest, but rather a race to see what has happened. Mary Magdalene has come and said, *They have taken away the Lord out of the tomb, and we do not know where they have taken Him* (John 20:2b).

The distance to the tomb is not far, but there is enough time for thoughts to race through their minds. Peter starts thinking like Peter again—his accusing mind sorting through the list of possibilities—including the likely perpetrators. *Who took Him, and where have they taken Him, and how are we going to get His body back?* Peter's mind is at full throttle. John is more methodical with his thoughts, trying to imagine what things look like at the tomb and also in the tomb. They say little as they approach the burial place of Jesus.

With a hurried hesitancy, they look inside—then enter the tomb. Peter enters first, followed by John: *Then the other disciple, who came to the tomb first, went in also; and he saw and believed. For as yet they did not know the Scripture, that He must rise again from the dead* (John 20:8).

They are alone. The guards are gone—headed to the city. There are no angels sitting around, ready to announce a Risen Savior. The quietness of the moment and the sacredness of the place grips both men, and they slowly move around inside the tomb, almost like the gentleness at a funeral.

The tomb is empty but for the folded linen clothes of Jesus. The blood—stained handkerchief from His head is folded and laying by itself. There is nothing else to see and nothing else to say. The body of Jesus is gone. *Then the disciples went away again to their own homes* (John 20:10).

Author's Comments

To understand the story that is unfolding this day, we must pause to reflect on John 20:8. We cannot simply blow past the words of John as he gives us amazing insight into the disciples' grasp of what these eight days mean on a spiritual and eternal level. We must be careful to grasp the mindset of those present two thousand years ago and not overlay the story with our understanding of the story today.

It is normal for us to think of Resurrection Sunday as a time of great rejoicing for Jesus has indeed risen from the dead. We sing Hallelujahs and we shout, "He is risen! He is risen! He is risen, indeed!" We do this with a significant understanding of the meaning of the resurrection. We understand why Jesus came; we grasp the spiritual significance of the Sacrificial Lamb; we have a level of understanding of the blood of Jesus—its power and how it covers our sin.

Therefore, we shout and rejoice and sing as we celebrate Resurrection morning: Christ has risen! He arose! Up from the grave He arose! He is alive! He is alive! Our joy is complete, for we know the meaning and the impact of the empty tomb.

But we do not read of those same reactions from the disciples at the tomb. We do not see the same excitement and joy and relief from the women or Peter or John. We do not see them dancing around, jumping up and down, or singing or rejoicing that Jesus has indeed risen and is alive.

For us, today, there is a theological understanding, revealed through the Bible, that unwraps the resurrection's meaning and significance. We get it. We understand the impact and the power of Jesus rising from the dead—the Conqueror of death and sin. We have been taught the fulfillment of prophecy these eight days have rendered. Our sins are blotted out—and we get it.

However, as the women stand at the entrance to the empty tomb, all they see is a body is missing—the body of their Lord. They do not understand where He had been taken or who has stolen His body. The words of the angels do little to soothe their spirit. They are afraid. Fear grips their entire being.

Repeatedly, the angels said to the women and the disciples, "Fear not," or "Do not be afraid." But fearful and afraid they are: *So they went out quickly and fled from the tomb, for **they trembled** and were amazed. And they said nothing to anyone, **for they were afraid*** (Mark 16:8). But it is not just the women who are fearful. The reaction of the disciples, later today, will be the same when Jesus appears to them where they are bolted in a room because of fear.

The fear of the guards, the fear of the Jews, the fear of a missing Lord, the fear of the unknown, the fear of the moment—all join forces to cause them to tremble. The events that are unfolding do not allow for theology or prophecy to be recognized or understood. These are uncertain days for the followers of Jesus, and they are not trying to digest teachings or prophecy.

It is easy to overlook the background of the disciples chosen by Jesus to be His apostles. They came not from the Sanhedrin—as Paul did. They were not educators or even highly educated. They mostly were fishermen, albeit accomplished fishermen. They would become incredibly faithful and dedicated followers of Jesus. But today, their faith—while present—is shallow, wobbling with each situation.

Most of all, there is no indication they are scholars of the Torah or the prophets. As Jesus teaches them about Himself—His purpose and His ministry—there is no foundation of studied scriptures for them to connect the dots. They heard Jesus say He would suffer at the hands of the chief priests, but they cannot connect the dots—if indeed, they can even see the dots. The men they will become, under the guidance of the Holy Spirit, are not the men they are today. Hence, we are given verse 8: *And he saw and believed. For as yet they did not know the scripture, that He must rise again from the dead.*

John says they saw and believed, but they did not understand. Many biblical scholars believe most of those missing dots Jesus connected for them when He spent time with them before His ascension—and well it may be.

However, as the fear of an empty tomb grips them, all the possibilities of what is happening race through their mind. Who has stolen the body of Jesus, and what is going to happen next? Because they do not know the scripture, they do not understand that Jesus has indeed risen from the dead!

They cannot see the risen Savior—all they see is a missing body. Therefore, there is no shouting and rejoicing yet. The enthusiasm we feel today on this Resurrection Sunday escapes them. But they will be singing and rejoicing in the coming days, and they will indeed go into the whole world and proclaim the gospel of a risen Jesus!

Mary Magdalene has followed Peter and John back to the tomb. She arrives after the two disciples have entered, simply standing outside the tomb weeping. Her thoughts are focused on the missing body of Jesus. The beauty of the garden that surrounds the tomb goes unnoticed. The birds chirping in the trees—bounding from tree to tree and seemingly cheering on the freshness and newness of the morning, are not heard. Even the fragrance of spring flowers fail to reach the senses of Mary Magdalene on this tenuous morning.

Mary is deeply grieving. Her efforts to cope with the horror of Friday and the numbness and the emptiness of yesterday have left her weak—and now this. Her plans to anoint the body of Jesus have been ripped from her and the other women—there is no body to anoint.

In silence, with soft sobs, she tries futilely to find answers to where they have taken Jesus's body. None of the possibilities in her mind are good. The words of the angel proclaiming, "He is not here. He has risen!" have failed to bring any meaning to Mary. All she sees is an empty tomb.

As Mary stands alone, there is a quietness that surrounds the tomb. Peter and John have left—returning home. She doesn't know what to do or think, so Mary slowly moves toward the tomb entrance and peers in—it just seems like the thing to do.

The words come in a soft, gentle, and compassionate voice: *Woman, why are you weeping? Whom are you seeking?* (John 20:15a). Jesus has just spoken to her, but Mary does not recognize Him—thinking He is a gardener. The response: *Sir, if You have carried Him away, tell me where You have laid Him, and I will take Him away* (John 20:15b). Mary is stressing over the missing body of Jesus.

But then comes the healing touch for a broken heart. It is the salve for a wound cut deep into the soul. It is what will make this dreadful morning become a bright and glorious morning—a resurrection morning!

Jesus says but one word: *Mary!* There are no questions of why she didn't recognize Him. There are no typical greetings given when friends meet. There is no "Are you glad to see Me?" There is but one word: "Mary!"

In John 10:27, Jesus says, *My sheep hear My voice, and I know them, and they follow Me.* Mary is a follower of Jesus. From that time in Galilee when Jesus cast out seven demons, Mary has been devoted to Jesus, and she knows His voice. One word—"Mary!" The word is not the miracle. It is the power behind the voice that is the miracle—the voice that comes from the lips of Jesus—the One who whispered, "Peace be still!" and the winds and the waves obeyed.

Suddenly, there is no need to search for a missing body. The fears of who stole the body of Jesus and what is next for the disciples is gone. Mary runs to Jesus, but Jesus tells her He has not yet ascended to the Father—do not cling to Me. She steps back from Him—her joy and excitement unabated. Then suddenly, Jesus is gone.

Jesus is gone – but His spirit remains with Mary. Her steps are no longer laborious as she almost bounds out of the tomb. The beauty of the morning grips her spirit, and the sound of the birds seem to be especially beautiful this morning. The voice of nature proclaiming a risen Savior is unmistakable. And the words of the angels are ringing in the ear of Mary:

"He is not here. He has risen!" Mary goes to tell the disciples that she has seen the Lord.

Jerusalem and the world are missing out on Resurrection morning. As the city stirs from its slumber, this day is just another day. The first day of the week brings all the normal activities—just like all the other first days of the week. The Sabbath always interrupts the work started the day before, but the work waits impatiently until the Sabbath is over. Jerusalem begins its normal routine.

Conversation is still springing up here and there concerning the Teacher and the discussions concerning His demise have people confused and wondering—depending on what you thought of Him. People are still trying to sort out the quake and the falling rock—most attributing them to normal seismic activity. However, the three hours of darkness are proving to be a bit more difficult to explain.

While on the surface things seem to be normal, the place of the crucifixion continues to draw the curious. People have heard the news of Friday's weird events, and they are walking to the hill of Golgotha to see the place for themselves. Some have come just to see what it looks like—others are seeking artifacts or souvenirs. Some uncomfortably climb the hill to see the holes where the base of the crosses stood or to see the blood stains on the ground. They wonder why around the middle cross the stains are so much larger. Wasn't that where the Teacher hung? Some pick up stones or dirt from the area. Someone found a single thorn stained with blood. However, the adversaries of Jesus have attempted to clear the area. They simply want Jerusalem to forget.

The people come and go throughout the day—just as they did yesterday. The volume is not large but steady nonetheless. Neighbors are angry with the activity. Friday was terrible—but can't people just stay away?

History will reveal the magnitude of this day, but just now, Jerusalem doesn't notice.

The road to Emmaus is not a flat seven-mile trek from Jerusalem nor is it just a path. Though not a rock star of biblical villages, Emmaus probably has a following for its "warm spring." Its dusty trail is shared by cart traffic as well as foot traffic. The deep ruts of carts reveal a busy and ancient road.

Emmaus is the destination of Cleopas and his friend, two disciples of Jesus. Why they are headed to Emmaus, we do not know. However, we do know Jesus is on their mind. Like all the other disciples, the events of the last few days are swirling through their minds and their conversation like a tornado. The reports of today, particularly, dominate their thoughts and words—a breached tomb, the body of Jesus missing, angels present at the tomb saying He is alive, the garments of Jesus folded and neatly placed on the hewn stone of the tomb and, mostly, the report of Mary Magdalene seeing and talking to Jesus himself.

The two walk along, frequently dodging carts, ruts, and the foot traffic moving at a more brisk and focused pace. The terrain is ever changing, frequently steep and occasionally treacherous. The disciples are too weary to offer a defiant challenge. They simply lower their heads and trudge along—their pace annoying the more robust.

With heads down and deep in thought, it takes a while before the men realize they have a third companion. The Man walks with them in silence, listening to their thoughts and reasoning as they walk and talk. They barely look up or even acknowledge the Man's presence. After a while, Jesus says to them, *What kind of conversation is this that you have with one another as you walk and are sad?* (Luke 24:17).

Their eyes are restrained, and they fail to recognize Jesus is walking by their side. So, they said to Him,

> *The things concerning Jesus of Nazareth, who was a Prophet mighty in deed and word before God and all the people, and how the chief priests and our rulers delivered Him to be condemned to death, and crucified Him.* **But we were hoping that it was He who was going to redeem Israel.** *Indeed, besides all this, today is the*

third day since these things happened. Yes, and certain women of our company, who arrived at the tomb early, astonished us. When they did not find His body, they came saying that they had also seen a vision of angels who said He was alive. And certain of those who were with us went to the tomb and found it just as the women had said; but Him they did not see.

– Luke 24:19b-24

Death on a cruel cross has not taken the Teacher out of Jesus. With gentleness, He calls them "foolish ones" and "slow in heart," and then Jesus begins to teach them about Himself—from Moses through all the prophets. *He expounds to them in all Scriptures the things concerning Himself* (verse 27b).

They have reached the village, and the two convince Jesus to spend the night with them. As they dine: *He took bread, blessed and broke it, and gave it to them. Then their eyes were opened and they knew Him; and He vanished from their sight* (Luke 24:30b-31).

You call Me Teacher and Lord, and you say well, for so I am (John 13:13).

It is evening in Jerusalem, and fear of the Jews still grips the apostles and disciples. The news about Jesus is slowly filtering through the city. The disciples are not saying much, except among themselves. But news always finds a way to spread. Maybe some of the information is being fed by the priests, scribes, and Pharisees. It certainly seems so, since most of the rumors say Jesus's disciples have stolen His body. However, His claims of rising from the dead are causing some to offer that as a possibility.

Meanwhile, as rumors spread throughout Jerusalem, the followers of Jesus are bolted in a room together, discussing a lot but mostly not knowing what to do. So, they retell their stories. They listen intently as first Mary Magdalene, then Peter and John and finally the two disciples, back from Emmaus, retell their story—every detail—one at a time. They listen, but they draw no conclusions or ideas of what they should do next. The Shepherd is gone, and the sheep are lost and confused.

Enter the Shepherd.

Jesus suddenly is standing in their midst. It is not a grand entry with lightning or the earth quaking to usher in His presence. There are no angels leading a procession nor trumpets sounding. Jesus is just there. The Shepherd joins His flock. With a calm and soft voice, Jesus says, *Peace to you* (Luke 24:36b). But fear is still their companion, and they think they are seeing a spirit. As fear envelops them, Jesus asks a question, *Why do doubts arise in your hearts? Behold My hands and My feet, that it is I Myself* (Luke 24:38-39a). The large scars of once present nails indeed confirm Jesus is standing before them in the flesh. He has indeed risen from the dead. A peace does indeed begin to relax their emotions. Jesus is here.

To further show He is in the flesh, Jesus asks for food. Luke tells us the menu items are broiled fish and some honeycomb. Jesus eats. The others eat also, albeit, most just stand and look at Jesus. *What does this all mean?* they wonder.

Jesus is not quite finished teaching His disciples. He begins by reminding them of all He told them during His ministry of the Law of Moses and the Prophets and the Psalms concerning Himself. Then *He opened their understanding, that they might comprehend the Scriptures* (Luke 24:35).

As Jesus leaves, faith has just taken a quantum leap. Understanding of the Messiahship of Jesus has replaced the hope of a Messiah to come defeat the Romans. The fulfillment of prophecy is comprehended, and the disciples are fast becoming those warriors who will tell the story of Jesus to the whole world.

Christ is risen! He is risen indeed! The Messiah has come, and we are indeed free—free from the shackles of sin. The whole room breaks out in joy as they laugh and sing the praises of a risen Savior. And Mary, the Mother of Jesus, sits and watches—so proud of her Son and Savior.

LIFE APPLICATION

But he said to them, "Do not be alarmed. You seek Jesus of Nazareth, who was crucified. He is risen! He is not here. See the place where they laid Him" (Mark 16:6).

Mary Magdalene told her story of seeing Jesus—but they did not believe. The disciples told their story of the Emmaus road—but they did not believe. When the disciples were gathered later that night, Jesus admonished them for their unbelief. Jesus told the two disciples they were slow of heart to believe.

Sometimes you and I are just like the disciples. The truth is there, but we struggle to believe it. We quickly believe gossip and social media posts which may be lies, but the truth we often struggle with. Why is that? Well, the answer, in part, is because Satan does not want you to know or believe the truth.

Question: What truth of God's Word are you struggling with? That He loves you? That He will forgive you? That He will always be with you? What must you do to increase your faith?

Some of the most powerful words spoken by the angel were *for He is risen, as He said.* "As He said"—these may be three of the most powerful words in the Bible. As He said. As who said? What is said is only as truthful as the one who said it. In this case, it is Jesus.

Question: Do you believe everything Jesus said? Every promise? Every statement about Himself? Do you cling to them? Do you stand on them? If you struggle in this area, begin to pray that God will allow you to believe—completely—without restraint—with full assurance. He will increase your faith as you ask Him and as you lean on His Word.

Chapter Twelve

> "Easter says you can put truth in a grave, but it won't stay there."
>
> Clarence W. Hall

For I know that my Redeemer lives (Job 19:25a).

Final Thoughts

As Jesus disappears, the apostles, and those gathered with them, look at each other as if to say, "Did you see what door He went out?" As quickly as He had appeared earlier, He also left. Where did He go? They do not know, but with His disappearance, it feels like the air has been sucked out of the room. They simply pause, glancing around with confused looks, and once again attempt to understand what has just happened.

Jesus had come and gone so quickly. But somehow, they sense they will see Him again soon. And indeed, they will. Jesus has more time on earth before He ascends to the Father. He will be seen by more than five hundred people over the next forty days. Eight days from now, He will again meet with the disciples. This time, Thomas is with them, and he will be encouraged by Jesus to touch His wounded side, saying, *Do not be unbelieving, but believing* (John 20:27b). Thomas replies, *My*

Lord and My God! (John 20:29). Jesus has proven He is alive—the risen Messiah!

In the coming days, Jesus will give the disciples what history calls the Great Commission: *"Go therefore and make disciples of all the nations, baptizing them in the name of the Father and of the Son and of the Holy Spirit, teaching them to observe all things that I have commanded you; and lo, I am with you always, even to the end of the age." Amen.* (Matthew 28:19-20).

It will be a charge that will be fulfilled with passion, compassion, and the power of the Holy Spirit. The eleven, plus Paul, plus the disciples, do indeed make disciples, and those disciples will make other disciples. And the Great Commission still marches on today.

In the coming days, empty fish nets will become overflowed with 153 fish: *And He said to them, "Cast the net on the right side of the boat, and you will find some." So they cast, and now they were not able to draw it in because of the multitude of fish . . . Simon Peter went up and dragged the net to land, full of large fish, one hundred and fifty-three; and although there were so many, the net was not broken* (John 21:6, 11).

On that same day, there will be a breakfast by the sea—the Sea of Galilee. *Jesus said to them, "Come and eat breakfast." . . . Jesus then came and took the bread and gave it to them, and likewise the fish* (John 21:12a, 13).

On that same day, at that same breakfast, Jesus will restore Peter with the instructions to *Feed My sheep* (John 21:17b). When Jesus asks Peter, *Do you love Me?* Peter replies, *Lord, You know all things; You know I love You* (John 21:17). And, indeed, Peter does love Jesus so! Peter will prove to be a faithful servant of Jesus. He will be a leader and an inspiration to the others. He will become a miracle worker and an orator of renown. Peter will indeed feed the sheep.

Forgiven are the three denials—those painful moments of weakness and shame. Forgiven are the moments of outspoken brashness—the times when Jesus rebuked Peter, even once saying to him, "Get behind Me, Satan!" Now, Jesus, in such a tender, yet powerful way, says to Peter, *Follow Me.* The message has not changed, for it was three years earlier, along these same shores, that Jesus said to Peter and Andrew, *Follow Me, and I will make you fishers of men. And they immediately left their nets and followed Him* (Matthew 4:19b-20).

On the pages of history will be recorded difficult times for Jerusalem following the eight days that changed the world. As Jesus revealed, the temple will be destroyed and the people will face years of oppression by the Romans. All that will be left standing of the Temple area will be the western wall or wailing wall. Not one stone of the Temple will remain.

The Messiah that the Jews are looking for to free them from the Romans will still be a weak but flickering hope. Conversely, the Messiah that Jeremiah, Isaiah, and the other prophets foretold in scripture has come and gone. Jerusalem, in her ignorance, has mostly missed Him.

The city is trying to return to normal following a most unusual Passover week. The chief priests, scribes, and Pharisees are still spreading their deceit about Jesus and His followers. They desperately work to squash the growth of Christianity. But they have failed to consider the power of the Holy Spirit, at work in the disciples, and Christianity is rapidly spreading. Paul will burst on the scene soon, and his missionary journeys will be used by God to spread the gospel to all nations.

Jerusalem is not able to rid itself of the imprint of these eight days. In the coming years and centuries, millions of people will come to visit the sights made famous or infamous by the events of this speck of time. The Via Delarosa, the Garden Tomb, the hill of Golgotha or Calvary, Caiaphas's Palace, the Mount of Olives, and certainly, the Garden of Gethsemane all will become must-see locations when people come to Jerusalem. New prayers will be offered in Gethsemane—maybe in the same spot Jesus prayed in such agony. People will sit on the Mount of Olives and gaze out over the city, just as Jesus did. Some may even weep for the city as well.

History will reveal the magnitude of this week and a day—these eight days. The wisdom and love wrapped into its days will be examined and proclaimed. But today, just now, Jerusalem is mostly unaware of what has happened to the spiritual canvas of time. The King has come; the Messiah has fulfilled His call; hope and faith have been rewarded; and man can proclaim with conviction and certainty, "It is well with my soul!"

The location is the Mount of Olives—a significant and special location in the story of Jesus and these eight days. And now, it will be the place where Jesus will ascend to be with the Father. Let us simply look at the words of Luke:

> *"Behold, I send the Promise of My Father upon you; but tarry in the city of Jerusalem until you are endued with power from on high." And He led them out as far as Bethany, and He lifted up His hands and blessed them. Now it came to pass, while He blessed them, that He was parted from them and carried up into heaven. And they worshiped Him, and returned to Jerusalem with great joy, and were continually in the temple praising and blessing God. Amen.*
>
> *– Luke 24:49-53*

LIFE APPLICATION

So Jesus said to them again, "Peace to you! As the Father has sent Me, I also send you" (John 20:21).

The story is not over. The story of these eight days has just begun because the hope for all sinful man began with a cross and an empty tomb. Jesus did not come, live, die, and arise for the movie line to say, "THE END." Jesus is alive, and therefore, hope is alive and salvation is available.

But as many as received Him, to them He gave the right to become children of God, to those who believe in His name (John 1:12).

This whole story is about people—people in the bondage of sin—people like you and me—people of the past, people of today, and people of tomorrow. All of us are sinners, and we desperately need a Savior. Please know and believe there is One. His name is Jesus, and He came to save His people from their sin. That includes you. That includes me.

These eight days fulfilled all of the needs of mankind—those who are broken and wrapped in the cocoon of sin—those who feel no hope—those who have tried and failed to figure it out on their own, and now, they despair because hope has vanished.

The forgiving power of the blood of Jesus did not vanish with Him as He ascended to heaven. The stories of these eight days are not the entirety of the stories. They are but the first.

The story is still being written, and the individual stories of today are just as amazing and dramatic as the stories written in the Bible. As He did with Mary Magdalene, Jesus is casting out demons today—demons of addiction, hate, and abuse. People whose lives were a train wreck are being transformed by the love of Jesus. Ask someone their story—their God story—and you will know the story of salvation and hope is still being written. Are you part of that story?

Notes

Introduction

1. **Bishop Michael Jarrell** – an American prelate of the Roman Catholic Church who served as the sixth bishop of the Roman Catholic Diocese of Lafayette in Louisiana until his resignation on February 18, 2016.

Chapter One

2. **Paul Ramsey** – an American Christian ethicist of the 20th century. He was a Methodist and graduated from Yale University. He taught Christian Ethics at Princeton University until the end of his life in 1988.

Chapter Two

3. **Peter Marshall** – a Scots-American preacher, pastor of the New York Avenue Presbyterian Church in Washington, DC and was appointed as Chaplain of the United States Senate.

4. **Hudson Taylor** – a British Protestant Christian missionary to China and founder of the China Inland Mission.

Chapter Three

5. **Henry Hart Milman** – an English historian and ecclesiastic.

6. **Song – "Wonderful Peace"** – a song by Warren D. Cornell & William G Cooper, 1889

7. **Strong's Exhaustive Concordance of the Bible** – an index of every word in the King James Version (KJV), constructed under the direction of James Strong.

<u>Chapter Four</u>

8. **Edwin Louis Cole** – the founder of the Christian Men's Network, an American religious organization devoted to helping Christian men and fathers.

<u>Chapter Five</u>

9. **James Stuart** – a minister of the Church of Scotland and theologian at the University of Edinburgh.

10. **Socrates** – a Greek philosopher from Athens and one of the founders of Western philosophy

<u>Chapter Six</u>

11. **Matthew Henry** – a nonconformist minister and author. He is best known for the six-volume biblical commentary Exposition of the Old and New Testaments.

12. **Song – "Sweet Hour of Prayer"** – Poem William Walford – 1842; Music William Bradbury – 1861

13. **Don Stewart** – a theologian and apologist and Calvary Chapel pastor.

14. **Website: inspired2think** – Article: "Understanding the significance of Jesus being anointed by oil" (11 April 2015).

<u>Chapter Seven</u>

15. **Phillip Yancey** – an American author who writes primarily about spiritual issues. His books have sold more than fifteen million.

16. **Strong's Exhaustive Concordance of the Bible** – see #7

17. **William Hendriksen** – a New Testament scholar and writer of Bible commentaries.

Chapter Eight

18. **Aiden Wilson Tozer** – an American Christian pastor, author, magazine editor, and spiritual mentor.

19. **Who's Who in The Bible** – a comprehensive book of people in the Bible by Joan Comay & Ronald Brownrigg, 1980.

20. **Rick Nerud** – Pastor at Calvary Chapel, St. George, Utah. Nerud has been at CCSG since 1997.

Chapter Nine

21. **C. H. Spurgeon** – an English preacher and pastor. Pastored Metropolitan Tabernacle for 38 years. Extensive author.

22. **Matthew Henry** – see #11

23. **International Standard Bible Encyclopedia** – an exhaustive Biblical encyclopedia – published in 1939.

24. **Alford Edersheim** – a Jewish convert to Christianity and a Biblical scholar known especially for his book The Life and Times of Jesus the Messiah – 1883.

25. **E.G. Lewis** – a noted author, his series on "The Seed of Christianity" became best sellers.

26. **Dr. Ralph F. Wilson** – a pastor, writer, artist and publisher, he is the director of Joyful Heart Renewal Ministries.

27. **Song – "Lonely Road, Up Calvary's Way** – a song by W. Elmo Mercer.

Chapter Ten

28. **Pastor Roger Steven Warner** – Lead Pastor of Brockton, Massachusetts Assembly of God.

29. **Pastor Gerrit Scott Dawson** – Pastor of First Presbyterian Church, Baton Rouge, Louisiana. He is also an aurthor.

Chapter Eleven

30. **Tim Keller** – an American pastor, theologian, Christian apologist and noted author.

Chapter Twelve

31. **Clarence W. Hall** – author of 59 works in seven languages.

CPSIA information can be obtained
at www.ICGtesting.com
Printed in the USA
FSHW021412240122